$4.00
BMW '20

Stories from the Great
METROPOLITAN
OPERAS

BY HELEN DIKE
Illustrated by Gustaf Tenggren

Officially Sponsored by the Metropolitan Opera Guild, Inc.

RANDOM HOUSE · NEW YORK

Escamillo has arrived, and with him is Carmen.

July 2016

Dear Don –

But our opera group
has wonderful great opera
stories to tell also. ALL IN APRIL
at The Metropolitan Opera House

<u>2011</u> Juan Diego Flores
assisted his wife in The delivery
of Their first child, in a water
bath, on The Upper West Side
30 minutes before The start
of The Comte Ory

<u>2013</u> Danielle De Niese
suddenly appeared in place
of Natalie Dessay in
Julio Cesare as Cleopatra.

<u>2016</u> In The last act of OThello
Aleksandrs Antonenko lost his
voice & The understudy Francesco
Anile sang at The side of The stage
in sneakers & jeans.

Contents

Get well soon
Love Mary (Palmer)

Foreword

EACH OF the twenty-five operas which are presented in this volume under the sponsorship of the Metropolitan Opera Guild has won its place in the affection of the public. In the history of our own Metropolitan Opera House *Aïda* heads the list, with more than three hundred performances. *Lohengrin* is a close second, with *Faust, Die Walküre, Pagliacci, Tristan,* and *Tannhäuser* following in popularity through the years.

Other works, such as *Orfeo, Fidelio, The Bartered Bride,* and *Don Giovanni,* appear less often in our active repertory, but they stand, nevertheless, as landmarks in the history of the art. Every one of these twenty-five operas offers to its audience a unique experience: it has achieved its fame by reason of a close appeal to the heart and mind. Not only in the music may be found the secret of its success. Look for it also in the drama of the story, in the personality of the characters. Each of them has some charm or power that makes for greatness; each has also some human quality that wins our personal friendship.

And so, in writing a word to introduce *Stories from the Great Metropolitan Operas* as one of the collection of books that I consider indispensable on the opera shelf, I wish to welcome its readers into a great company of fascinating people. Here is your invitation into the brilliant court of ancient Egypt, into the band of passionate smugglers in the Spanish mountains, into the peasant festivals of Sicily and Bohemia and the very human gathering of the Norse gods!

Soon, perhaps, you will wish to hear the speech of your new friends, to witness a great musical performance where the opera will live for you by tone and picture as well as plot. When you enter the doors of the Metropolitan Opera House you will be most welcome. Through the Junior Performances of the Metropolitan Opera Guild nearly 50,000 young people, with the co-operation of their schools, have been enabled to witness opera. We look to you as our audience of the future.

And, meanwhile, may this book lead you along a happy path to the world of opera!

EDWARD JOHNSON
General Manager,
Metropolitan Opera Association.

Aïda

BY GIUSEPPE VERDI

*Libretto by Antonio Ghislanzoni, after a sketch by
Mariette Bey and the French text of Camille du Locle*

PRINCIPAL CHARACTERS (*in order of appearance*):

Ramfis (bass), high priest of the Temple of Isis.

Radames (tenor), a brilliant young soldier, captain of the Egyptian guard.

Amneris (mezzo-soprano), haughty and self-willed daughter of the King of Egypt,
in love with Radames.

Aïda (soprano), an Ethiopian maiden taken prisoner in war, now the slave of
Amneris.

King of Egypt (bass).

Amonasro (baritone), savage King of Ethiopia, and father of Aïda, whose rank is
unknown to her captors.

PLACE: Memphis and Thebes, in Egypt.   TIME: The reign of the Pharaohs.

THE PRELUDE opens softly with a tender, yearning melody, the theme
of Aïda:

It is interrupted by the relentless tread of a second melody, representing
the priesthood of Egypt, which guards the glory of the nation:

But even as this gathers volume, the pleading note of Aïda returns and mingles with the march of the priests, as though thoughts of fame and of love were struggling in the mind of the hero, Radames.

ACT ONE, *Scene One*. The curtain rises on a portico in the palace of the King at Memphis. At the right is a curtained entry, in the distance the colonnades of the palace thrust into the blue sky. The high priest, Ramfis, is talking with the young captain of the guard.

"Ethiopian hordes are again invading our country," he declares, "and the goddess Isis has named a warrior to lead our forces against them. I must hasten to tell the King of her decree." Radames gazes after the departing priest with flashing eyes.

"If only the choice might fall on me!" he exclaims. "O, beloved Aïda, I would fight and conquer for you alone. . . ."

His thoughts are interrupted by the princess Amneris, who has followed the young warrior. She notes his flushed look. and, instantly suspicious, asks who has made him so happy. Radames tells her of his military aspirations. But the sudden entrance of Aïda draws a startled exclamation from him.

"Can she be my rival?" wonders the Princess. "Ah, tremble, slave, if this is your secret." Then, turning to Aïda, she assures her of sisterly love. "Why do you weep?" she asks.

Aïda laments the fate of her unhappy country.

Radames fears the Princess has discovered his love for her slave.

A fanfare heralds the approach of the King, who enters surrounded by his guards and followed by Ramfis and the priests. He calls upon the Egyptians to fling back the invaders. Led by their warrior-king, Amonasro, the Ethiopians are even now marching on Thebes, burning and pillaging.

Enraged, the crowd shouts for vengeance. The King turns to Radames.

"Isis has named you leader of our forces," he proclaims. "Go forth to victory."

"All glory to the gods in whose hands your fate rests," cries the high priest, and, as Amneris gives Radames the banner of Egypt, bidding him return victorious, all hasten off to the Temple of Vulcan. Aïda is left alone.

"Return victorious!" she echoes, horrified. "Shall I wish the downfall of my father and brothers who fight to set me free? O gods, destroy the squadrons of Egypt! . . . But can I forget Radames, whose tenderness has lightened the dark hours of my slavery? Ah, kind Heaven, have pity on me."

Scene Two. The interior of the Temple of Vulcan is half lost in the smoke of incense. Long rows of columns vanish in the darkness, while from above a mysterious light falls on the altar with its carved images of the gods. Ramfis stands before the altar, priests and priestesses surrounding him. From within the inner sanctuary come the sound of harps and the voice of the high priestess. "Almighty Phthah," she chants. "We invoke you."

Radames appears. Unarmed, he advances to the altar, and, while the priestesses sway in mystic dance, Ramfis gives him the sacred armor. "Defend the soil of Egypt, O god," cries the high priest:

"Lend me your strength," Radames implores. As the priests lift their voices in praise, the weird song of the high priestess again echoes through the temple.

THE SECOND ACT, *Scene One*, opens on a terrace in the apartments of Amneris. Reclining on her couch, the Princess is being adorned for the triumphal return of the Egyptian armies. "Our foe is vanquished," sing the slaves as they weave flowers into her headdress. "Let love reward the victor."

The Princess is dreaming of Radames. But, seeing Aïda approach, she dismisses her servants. Is the Ethiopian maiden her rival in love, she wonders? The thought tortures her. So, pretending to be a friend, she sympathizes with Aïda's sorrow at the defeat of her countrymen. "Time will cure your grief," she promises. "And love will make you happy again."

"Love!" Aïda is startled.

"Have you lost some friend on the battlefield?" the Princess asks. Then, noting the girl's confusion and anxiety, she tells her Radames has fallen.

"Radames slain!" Aïda cries in despair.

Amneris faces her with flashing eyes. "No. I have deceived you. He lives. But lie no more, slave. You love him. Well, I am your rival—I, daughter of the King of Egypt."

For an instant Aïda confronts her proudly. She too is a princess. . . . Just in time she stops herself and, bowing humbly, begs for pity. "I cannot live without him," she whispers.

Amneris spurns her plea furiously. Then, as a hymn of triumph echoes through the palace, she sweeps from the chamber.

Aïda sinks to her knees. "Pity, kind Heaven," she implores. "Give me release in death."

Scene Two. Cheering crowds throng the entrance to the city of Thebes. The victorious Egyptian armies are returning, and the people wave their garlands before the Temple of Ammon and around the great canopied throne that has been erected on the right. Presently the King enters and seats himself under the dais with Amneris at his side.

The sound of trumpets is heard:

"Hail to our warriors, hail to the victor," shout the people, strewing flowers in the roadway. Then the troops pass through the great triumphal arch at the rear. Banners, sacred vessels, and images of the gods are borne past, dancing girls bring the spoils of the defeated. Finally Radames appears in a war chariot, greeted by the cheers of the crowd. He is saluted by the King, who promises to grant any request that the hero may make, and Amneris crowns him with the laurel wreath of victory.

Then the captives are summoned. Laden down with chains they stagger in. Among them is a tall, defiant warrior.

"My father," gasps Aïda.

"Don't betray me," Amonasro whispers, embracing her, and he tells the King that he is an officer of the Ethiopian monarch, whom he saw perish on the field of battle. "We are defeated and leaderless, O King," he cries. "Have mercy on us."

The other slaves and the people also plead for mercy; Ramfis and the priests oppose them bitterly. At length, touched by the misery of Aïda, Radames asks the King to fulfill his vow to give him anything he wishes by freeing the prisoners.

"The request is granted," replies the King, "but for your services to Egypt I give you also a more priceless reward—the hand of Amneris."

"Glory to Isis and to Egypt," shout the people exultantly. The King descends from his throne, and, flushed with triumph, Amneris follows, accompanied by the despairing Radames. Aïda and her father are left alone.

"Take courage," he whispers to the heart-broken girl. "Vengeance is at hand."

ACT THREE, *Scene One.* Palm trees hang over the banks of the Nile, and half hidden among them stands the Temple of Isis. It is night. Silently a boat draws up to the shore. On the eve of her wedding, Amneris has come to pray for the love of Radames, and, together with the high priest, she makes her way through the silvery moonlight to the temple. From within comes the solemn chant of the guardians of the sanctuary.

As the sacred portals close behind her, Aïda slips out of the shadows. "Radames will meet me here," she whispers. "Ah, if he fails me, then let the waters of the Nile bring oblivion." Her thoughts turn to her native land, which she may never see again:

Suddenly Amonasro appears at her side. He has come on a grave mission. Reminding her of the Ethiopian temples profaned by the Egyptians, of the innocent women and children killed, he tells her that her people are again in arms. They await word of the road the enemy will take. She must discover it for them . . . from Radames, the Egyptian leader, her lover.

Horrified, Aïda shrinks back. "No, never! I cannot."

"So this is your love for your country," Amonasro responds savagely. "Up then, Egyptian legions! Destroy us with fire and sword."

He flings the poor girl from him. "Never call yourself my daughter. The Ethiopian dead cry to you! They will haunt you! Your own mother will curse you!"

In terror Aïda promises to obey him, and, as Radames enters, the Ethiopian King conceals himself in the shrubbery.

"O, the joy of seeing you again, beloved," cries the young man ardently. But Aïda repulses him. He belongs to Amneris.

"I love you alone," he protests, and tells her that after the coming battle he will ask the King for her hand.

"Will that shield us from the vengeance of Amneris or from the fury of the priests?" she replies sadly. "No, only one way remains. We must flee. In the groves and valleys of my native land we can find happiness."

He sweeps her into his arms. "Yes, let us flee."

But, as they hasten off, Aïda pauses. "What road shall we take to avoid the Egyptian armies?"

"The Pass of Napata," answers Radamés.

Amonasro springs from his place of hiding. "There my men shall attack," he cries triumphantly. "And I, Amonasro, shall lead them."

Radames turns in horror. "I have betrayed my country. O gods! . . ."

At that moment Amneris and Ramfis appear upon the temple steps. "Traitor," cries the Princess. The guards rush forward, but Aïda and her father slip away into the night. Radames surrenders his sword to the high priest.

THE FOURTH ACT, *Scene One*, opens on a corridor in the palace, where Amneris cowers, waiting for Radames to be led to trial.

At last the prisoner enters.

"Save yourself," the Princess implores him. "Declare your innocence, and I will beg for mercy from the King."

But he scorns to defend himself. "Then live for my love," she pleads.

"You have killed Aïda," Radames responds. "Take my life, too."

"Aïda lives," Amneris tells him bitterly. "She disappeared after the battle in which her father was slain. Renounce her, and I will save you."

"Never!" he replies. Overcome with jealousy, the Princess signals the guards to advance.

The priests cross the hall, leading Radames away.

"Almighty gods, defend him. He is innocent!" cries Amneris in despair.

From below come the voices of the priests. "Radames, Radames, defend yourself."

"He is silent," cries Ramfis.

"He is a traitor," echo the priests. "Let him be buried alive."

The procession returns from the judgment chamber. Vainly Amneris hurls her curses upon them.

Scene Two. Radames has been thrust into a vault beneath the altar in the glittering Temple of Vulcan. Two priests are closing the entrance to his tomb. "O, my Aïda," cries the doomed man, as the last gleam of light is shut out. "I shall never see your dear face again."

Suddenly he hears a faint groan, a form stirs in the darkness. It is Aïda. "I wanted to die in your arms," she whispers, in answer to his startled questions.

Above them the priestesses move in ritual dance before the altar, chanting their song of worship. "Listen, beloved. It is our hymn of death. . . ." Desperately Radames tries to move the stone of the vault. His efforts are in vain; the lovers bid farewell to the world:

Amneris appears in the Temple. Bowed with grief, she throws herself upon the stone which entombs the man she loves, and, as Radames and Aïda sink to the ground in the darkness below, she prays to Isis for peace.

"Almighty Phthah, we invoke you," chant the priests. The curtain falls.

The Barber of Seville

BY GIOACCHINO ROSSINI

*Libretto by Sterbini, adapted from the
celebrated French play of Beaumarchais*

PRINCIPAL CHARACTERS *(in order of appearance)*:

Count Almaviva (tenor), a young nobleman who, having once caught a glimpse of
Rosina, has fallen in love with her and serenades her every morning, hoping
to find an opportunity of exchanging a word with the girl.

Figaro (baritone), barber of Seville.

Rosina (soprano), a lovely but wilful young girl.

Dr. Bartolo (bass), guardian of Rosina. Suspicious and jealous, the old doctor
keeps his ward locked in her room.

Don Basilio (bass), a meddling scandalmonger and friend of Dr. Bartolo. He is
Rosina's music teacher.

PLACE: Seville, in Spain.   TIME: The seventeenth century.

ACT ONE. After a lively overture, the curtain rises on a street in Seville
outside the house of Dr. Bartolo. Day is breaking. From the shadows

tiptoes a band of musicians led by Fiorello, a servant of the young Count
Almaviva. They place themselves under a window opening on a balcony.

A few minutes later Almaviva strides down the alley. He greets the
men briefly and turns to the window above. As the musicians strike up an
accompaniment on their guitars he sings a tender love song: "The dawn
is breaking—one smile from you is all my delight."

Within the house all is silent and dark. Almaviva arouses himself from
the revery into which he has slipped. "Music cannot help me," he murmurs. He gives Fiorello money for the men, who, overjoyed at his kind-
ness, crowd around thanking him noisily. Fiorello drives them away with
difficulty. At last the count is alone.

He looks up at the window. "I will win you. . . ." he begins. But he is
interrupted abruptly.

"La-la-la." sings a merry voice. The count slips under an archway as a
tall, jovial fellow enters, singing gaily and accompanying himself on a
guitar slung around his shoulders by a broad ribbon.

"I am the handy man of Seville." he cries.

"Needed by everyone—paupers or patrons, maidens or matrons. Figaro?
I am here. Figaro? I am there. . . ."

He breaks off with a laugh. "What a life! Not a girl in Seville ever gets
married without my help."

The count has been listening with interest and now he comes forward.
Figaro recognizes him. "Your Lordship."

"Not so loud, friend," cautions Almaviva, and he tells the barber about
his love for the maiden.

"Why, what luck!" answers Figaro. "In that house I am barber, bot-
anist, leech, and hairdresser." The door opens, and quickly the two slip
into hiding.

Dr. Bartolo comes out. "If Don Basilio comes, tell him to wait." he calls fretfully, locking the door behind him. "I must attend today to my marriage with Rosina."

"His marriage with Rosina," echoes the count as the doctor hobbles away. "Then we must hurry."

Figaro suggests another serenade. Rosina is listening, he is sure.

Fired by this thought, the young man borrows his companion's guitar and places himself boldly under the window. "My name is Lindoro," he sings. "I am poor in possessions, but rich in love for you, dearest."

A girl's voice answers: "Rosina gladly gives Lin—" The window is slammed violently.

"O, fury!" cries the count; then, turning to the barber, he implores his aid. "You must think of some way to open the door for me. I will reward you richly."

"You can't imagine how the promise of gold has sharpened my wits," responds Figaro. "Ah, I have it! A regiment has arrived today. You must dress up as a soldier and claim to be billeted in the doctor's house. How is that for an invention?—Bravo, bravo, Figaro!" he applauds himself gaily. "Then if you pretend to be tipsy the old man won't be suspicious of what you do."

Almaviva is delighted with the scheme.

ACT TWO takes place in Rosina's apartment. The girl has just written a letter, and sits musing on the youth who sang beneath her window.

She loves him, and vows that all her guardian's efforts will not keep her from her Lindoro. "How shall I send him this note?" she wonders, then remembers that she saw the young man talking to Figaro.

At that moment the barber enters. He has barely time to whisper that he has news and slip from the room when in stumps old Dr. Bartolo.

"That barber!" he sputters. "Have you been talking to him?"

"And why not?" replies his ward pertly, as she leaves.

Bartolo is furious, but before he can follow the girl the door opposite is flung open and in stalks Don Basilio, a large umbrella in one hand. "I have news," he croaks. "Count Almaviva is in town."

"What?" shrieks the doctor in dismay. "The villain who has been serenading my Rosina? We must act, Don Basilio."

"Yes, but on the sly," answers the other craftily. He looks around to make sure they are alone, and Figaro, who has been listening at the door, pops out of sight. "Ruin his reputation and we will chase our gallant out of Seville," Basilio suggests.

But the doctor is impatient. Slander will take too long. No, he must marry the girl tomorrow. The conspirators go off to prepare a contract.

"So that's the way the wind blows," chuckles Figaro in the doorway. Rosina comes in and he tells her what he has discovered.

She laughs at the notion of marrying her uncle, then questions Figaro about the young man she saw him talking to beneath her window.

"O, he is a distant cousin of mine," answers the barber airily. "A clever fellow, but in love just now with a young lady of Seville."

"Is she pretty?" asks Rosina slyly. "And what is her name?"

Figaro makes a deep bow. "R-o, ro, s-i, si. n-a, na!"

"Now you are deceiving me," she says reproachfully, but when he asks her for a few lines to give her lover, she shows him the note.

"What!" he cries in amazement. "Already written. O. you women!" Off he runs with the letter just as Dr. Bartolo returns.

"What was the barber saying to you?" the old man asks suspiciously. "I'll wager he brought a letter." Suddenly he seizes the girl's hand. "Aha, just as I thought. Ink on your finger. And why is a sheet of paper missing from the desk? And how does it happen that the pen is newly cut?"

Rosina hesitates. She burnt her finger, she replies. and dipped it in the ink to heal it. She used the paper for wrapping and the pen to trace a flower on her embroidery.

"You fibber!" shouts Dr. Bartolo. and. becoming more and more excited, he threatens her with immediate marriage. At last he stamps out of the room, followed by his niece.

"Why you are pale as a ghost, Don Basilio."

A loud knocking is heard at the door. The maid, Bertha, goes to open it. but a minute later she comes flying back. After her staggers a drunken soldier. "Ho, there, within," he shouts, thumping with his sword. It is Count Almaviva in disguise.

Dr. Bartolo enters hastily. "What is all this?" he demands.

The intruder flourishes an order; he has been quartered at the doctor's house. Furious, the old man protests that he is exempt. Rosina slips into the room.

"Go to your chamber, Miss," he shrieks at her, but she manages to exchange a word with her lover as the old man searches frantically for a permit which relieves him of housing soldiers. "Here you are," he cries at last, producing a paper.

The count knocks it out of his hand with his sword. "Will you fight?" he demands, and as he dances about Bartolo he drops a note on the floor for Rosina.

The doctor has seen the ruse. "Give me that letter," he screams. Rosina deftly exchanges a laundry bill for the note.

At that moment in rush Basilio and Bertha the housekeeper, followed by Figaro. "Half Seville is outside," shouts the barber.

A violent knocking is heard. The guard has come to investigate the disturbance; Almaviva is arrested. But drawing the officer in charge to one side, the count reveals who he is. At once the officer falls back respectfully. To the amazement of everyone, especially Dr. Bartolo, who stands rooted to the floor, the young man is released.

ACT THREE. Seated in the same room, Dr. Bartolo ponders on the identity of the soldier, of whom he has at length rid himself. "I'll wager he was sent by Count Almaviva," he exclaims angrily. His thoughts are interrupted by a knock at the door.

"Come in," the doctor calls, then stares in astonishment. There stands a music master in the black gown of the church.

"Peace be with you," he mumbles, bowing.

"I am a pupil of Don Basilio, who is ill."

Dr. Bartolo is uneasy. His guest has a strangely familiar look. But when the man produces a letter written by Rosina which he claims to have found in the count's lodgings, and offers to blacken the young man's reputation with Bartolo's niece, the old man hurries off in delight to fetch her.

A few minutes later he returns with Rosina. "This gentleman will give you your lesson this morning," he announces.

The girl gives a start of surprise; she recognizes her lover.

"Now what will you sing, young lady?" asks the count, sitting down at the piano. Rosina sings an aria.

Bartolo is bored. "A tiresome ditty," he complains, and sings a song of his own, while Figaro, who has come in with his shaving things, imitates him from behind.

Suddenly the old man turns around. "Well, what have you come for?"

The barber pretends to be astonished. "Why to shave you, of course. And it can't be put off. My schedule is full." The doctor agrees reluctantly, and, giving Figaro his keys, sends him after towels.

From outside comes a tremendous crash.

"Knave!" shrieks Bartolo, and rushes out. The lovers are alone. Hastily they exchange a word of love; then Bartolo returns, followed by Figaro, who has made use of the excitement to secure the key to Rosina's window. Now, free to work, he tucks a towel under the doctor's chin, lathers his face, and with a flourish of his razor is about to begin when the door opens and in walks Don Basilio.

The count thinks quickly. "What do you mean by coming out with a fever?" he exclaims. "Why you are as pale as a ghost."

"Yes, and shaking like a leaf," adds Figaro. They press a purse into Basilio's hand, to the fellow's astonishment. All urge him to go home to bed, and after much delay he finally departs.

Figaro goes on with his shaving. He attempts to distract Bartolo's attention while the count whispers to Rosina that they will come for her at midnight. But the doctor is suspicious. Rising, he steals unnoticed behind the lovers and suddenly thrusts himself between them. "Scoundrels," he shouts furiously, chasing them about the room. At last Figaro and the count escape into the street, and Rosina flees to her room. The doctor departs in search of Don Basilio.

"What a madhouse!" sighs Bertha, as she begins to right the upturned furniture. "This love is a crazy thing." She goes out.

Night has come on, and outside a violent storm rages. Suddenly the shutters are flung back. Figaro and the count climb through the window, and a minute later Rosina joins them. Almaviva attempts to embrace her, but the girl repulses him. Her uncle has shown her the letter she wrote to Lindoro, which was found in the count's lodgings. Convinced of her lover's faithlessness. she has come to unmask him.

"But I am Almaviva," cries the count. "Lindoro is only a name."

Figaro interrupts them. "We must be off," he urges, drawing them to the window. The ladder is gone.

While they are wondering what to do Don Basilio bursts into the room bringing a notary to marry Dr. Bartolo and his niece. Almaviva slips the music teacher a ring. "Here is a trifle for you." he whispers. "Or if that doesn't suit you, I have a bullet for your head." Then, with Don Basilio and Figaro as witnesses, the lovers sign the wedding contract. In hurries Dr. Bartolo with the guard.

"Arrest the thieves," he shouts, but he is too late. Rosina is a countess. There is nothing left for the old doctor to do but forgive his wilful niece, and join the others in wishing joy to the happy couple.

The Bartered Bride

BY BEDŘICH SMETANA

Libretto by K. Sabina

PRINCIPAL CHARACTERS *(in order of appearance):*

Jenik (tenor), a young peasant from another neighborhood, who has made his home in the village where Marie lives.

Marie (soprano), daughter of Kruschina and Ludmila. She is deeply in love with Jenik, and is loved in return by the handsome stranger, whose past history is a mystery to everyone in the village.

Kezal (bass), the village marriage broker.

Kruschina (baritone), a prosperous peasant.

Ludmila (soprano), his wife.

Vashek (tenor), son of Tobias Micha by a second marriage.

Tobias Micha (bass), a wealthy landowner from the region near the Moldau River.

Hata (mezzo-soprano), his shrewish second wife.

PLACE: A Bohemian village.   TIME: A feast day, about 1850.

THE OVERTURE begins with a wild and brilliant tune:

It whirls down the scale and into a rugged second theme:

This, in turn, races up and down the scale until finally it bursts into a joyous folk-song melody:

ACT ONE. The curtain rises on a village square, gay with wreaths and garlands and the colored streamers of a maypole. At either side cluster quaint wooden houses. In the back, the road passes the church, crosses a bridge, and winds up a hillside. The village girls have bright aprons over their skirts and ribbons in their hair, the peasants have polished boots, and as they dance all sing gaily of the danger of falling in love in the spring.

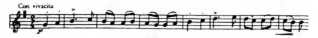

But Marie is sad. Her father has arranged for her to marry the son of rich Tobias Micha, and today the unknown bridegroom is coming to see her. "What shall I do?" she asks Jenik. "You are the one I love."

Jenik laughs her fears away. He tells her of his youth, and how he was driven from his father's house by an unkind stepmother. "Now, dearest, *you* will have to make a home for me."

Marie throws herself into his arms. Joyously they promise to love each other forever:

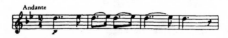

Just then Marie sees her father approaching, and the lovers slip away as Kezal, the marriage broker, hustles Kruschina and his wife across the square. The three sit down at a table. Kezal signals for beer, chattering all the while about the wonderful bargain he has made for Kruschina.

Ludmila thinks it would be a good idea for Marie to see her bridegroom before the agreement is finally settled, but she is overruled. "No need for that," sputters Kezal impatiently. "Why, the boy is a wonder. Perfectly mannered, sober, timid, the envy of every mother. You will see, the young folks will fall in love the minute they meet."

While Kruschina and Ludmila are exclaiming over the unusual qualities of their future son-in-law, Marie returns.

"Now, my pretty child," says Kezal coaxingly. "What do you suppose I have for you? A fine young man!"

"Let the fine young man look for someone else," Marie retorts. "Jenik and I have sworn to give each other our hearts."

"What?" shouts Kruschina. "Without my consent? Why, I have promised you to Micha's son." Kezal pulls out the contract. "There you are, Miss, in black and white, signed and witnessed."

Marie strikes the paper out of his hand. "Was I present when you signed it?" she demands. "Then it is no good at all." She goes off.

"It was a great mistake not to bring Vashek along to woo her," Kruschina laments, but Kezal reassures him. "You talk to Father Micha over there in the inn. I will attend to Jenik."

The peasants crowd into the square. Some sit down at the tables and order beer, others dance a gay polka:

"If we could have our way, the whole world would dance with us," they sing exuberantly.

ACT TWO. Jenik and a crowd of young peasants are drinking in the inn. "Heissassa! foaming beer," shout the revelers, waving their mugs in the air, "a man gets fire and strength from you. Nothing else matters." Jenik thinks that to love and be loved is better yet.

"What good is love if you have no gold?" retorts old Kezal, who is sitting by himself at the other side of the room. He approaches Jenik confidingly, but at that moment the village maidens flock into the room. Leaving their beer, the peasants join the girls in a wild Bohemian national dance called the Furiant:

Breathless, all rush out-of-doors.

Presently Vashek, the son of Micha, enters. "M-m-m-my mother says it's t-t-time to get m-m-married." he stutters, looking about the empty room. "If I d-d-don't, everyone w-w-will laugh."

Marie comes in. She stops when she sees Vashek. "Aren't you Marie's betrothed?" she asks. Then, pretending deep admiration, she tells him that all the girls think it is a pity for such a handsome fellow to marry a creature like Marie. "She's in love with another man, you know," she explains. "She'll slander you behind your back, and make your life miserable." Poor Vashek is terrified.

"But I know another girl," Marie adds coquettishly, "who is just as pretty and young as I am, and she adores you."

"Really!" shouts Vashek joyfully. Marie urges him to renounce his betrothed. "This other girl will love you faithfully," she promises. Vashek swears to forget Marie. Then he tries to embrace his new-found love, but she slips away. He runs after her.

In bustles Kezal, dragging Jenik with him. "Everyone knows that Marie has won your heart," sputters the marriage broker, "but the question is, have you any money?" Jenik admits he hasn't much.

"What a tragedy!" groans his companion. "Then your happiness will never last. But I know just the wife for you, my boy—a fine wench with plenty of money, not to mention a house and garden, pigs and cows, pitchers and tubs. Why, even a prince would be glad to wed her."

Jenik is not interested. Kezal tries bribery. "I'll pay you three hundred gulden to give up Marie," he promises.

The young man ponders for a moment. "Very well," he agrees. "I will sign the contract. But only on condition that nobody but Micha's son shall have her." Delighted, Kezal rushes away to get witnesses.

"The blockhead," laughs Jenik, looking after him. "He fell right into my trap. Does he really suppose I would sell my love?"

A few minutes later the marriage broker returns with Kruschina and a mob of peasants. The contract is read aloud; then, to everyone's dismay, Jenik signs away his sweetheart.

THE THIRD ACT opens on the village square. Marie has slipped away from Vashek, and the poor fellow is terrified of what his mother will say to him. "Love is s-s-sad," he laments. But his woe is soon forgotten in the excitement of watching a band of strolling players who arrive in the square. The ringmaster announces a rehearsal and performance starring the beautiful Esmeralda. Tight-Rope Queen, an Indian chief named Murru, and a live bear from America.

Vashek is charmed by Esmeralda. He decides that she would make the right wife for him, and is busy assuring her that he will come to see her dance, when the Indian rushes in with terrible news. The man who takes the part of the bear has drunk himself into a stupor. Murru has been all over town, but nowhere has he found anybody to fit in the bear skin; one is too tall, the next too short. Suddenly his eye lights on Vashek. He is just the right size. Hastily the ringmaster and Esmeralda persuade Vashek to act the bear.

Vashek practices his dance. "All the g-g-girls l-l-love me," he sings happily. A clutch on the shoulder interrupts him. "What are you doing?" cries his mother angrily. "Come with us to meet your bride."

"Let go. I don't want M-m-m-marie," protests Vashek, as Kezal confronts him with the contract to sign. "She'll w-w-worry me to death," and, wrenching loose, he runs off. As they gaze after him in astonishment, Kruschina, Ludmila, and Marie join them. The girl cannot believe that her lover has betrayed her. "They are only inventing slander to separate us," she insists. Kezal shows her Jenik's signature.

At that moment Vashek returns. He is astonished to see Marie. "There is the g-g-girl who told me not to m-m-marry Marie."

"But that *is* Marie!"

"W-w-w-what!" shouts the booby, overjoyed, and he declares himself ready to marry. Poor Marie begs for a little time alone to think it over.

"How can I believe that Jenik is false?" she cries sadly, when all have left. "And yet there was his signature. O, the world is so dismal."

Jenik rushes in joyfully. Marie rebuffs his advances and tearfully demands the truth; did he sell her to Vashek or not?

"Well, I did sign the contract," he admits, laughing, "but if you will listen a minute. my dear. I'll tell you how it all came about. . . ."

"Not another word," she retorts angrily, and as Kezal returns she tells him she is willing to marry Vashek.

Kruschina and his wife and the parents of Vashek come out of the inn, followed by a crowd of peasants. Suddenly Jenik steps up to Tobias Micha and his wife, Hata. "Why, Jenik!" they cry in astonishment.

"Here I am. Father and Mother." replies the young man cheerily. "Yes," he continues to the others, "I too am Micha's son, long lost but hale and hearty!"

Kezal is bewildered. "Jenik—the son of Micha?" he echoes blankly.

"Yes, and ready to claim his bride. Which of us will you have, Marie?" Jenik asks tenderly. She runs to him. "I am yours forever, dearest."

Micha turns scornfully to the marriage broker: "A fine business man you turned out to be!" Followed by the hoots of the peasants, Kezal flees.

As he vanishes shouts are heard: "The bear has broken loose—run, run," and a brown furry creature lopes into the square. The people scatter in a panic.

"D-d-d-don't be afraid," cries a squeaky voice. "It's only V-v-vashek." Lifting off the head, the booby grins at the frightened peasants.

"O. you dunce." screams Hata furiously. "You will make a laughing stock of us." She hustles her son off.

Kruschina taps Tobias Micha on the shoulder. "You know, friend, I think Jenik is the best husband for Marie after all."

"Yes," adds Ludmila, "and you should be glad to get your boy back."

Micha laughs jovially. "Well, he may surely have my blessing."

As the happy couple kneels before him, the peasants joyfully wish long life and happiness to the 'bartered bride.'

Vashek swears to forget Marie.

Carmen

BY GEORGES BIZET

Libretto by Meilhac and Halévy,
adapted from Prosper Mérimée's novel

PRINCIPAL CHARACTERS *(in order of appearance):*

Micaela (soprano), a peasant girl from the countryside near Seville.

Don José (tenor), a hot-blooded young corporal of dragoons, stationed in Seville. He is in love with Micaela, his childhood sweetheart.

Zuniga (bass), the captain of Don José's company.

Carmen (mezzo-soprano), a bold and heartless gypsy who works in the cigarette factory. She is the ally of a band of smugglers hiding in the mountains near Seville.

Frasquita (soprano) }
Mercedes (contralto) } , gypsy friends of Carmen.

Escamillo (baritone), a toreador of Granada.

El Remendado (tenor) }
El Dancairo (baritone) } , leaders of the smugglers.

PLACE: Seville and the neighboring mountains.   TIME: About 1820.

THE PRELUDE begins with a brilliant military theme, suggesting soldier life in the barracks and squares of Seville:

It dies away, and a second melody appears—the rhythmic song of the toreador, as dashing in love as in the bull ring:

The military note returns, but it is cut off abruptly by a sombre, threatening motive—Fate:

ACT ONE. The curtain rises on a square in Seville near the cigarette factory. Corporal Morales and a group of soldiers lounge before the guardhouse at the left, watching the bustling, careless throng in the square. They notice a pretty young peasant girl. She is looking about shyly, as though in search of someone. Glad of a diversion, Morales offers to help her. "I am looking for Don José," she replies.

The officer tells her that José's watch will soon return to duty, and invites her to wait in the guardhouse. But the girl slips away.

A military band strikes up, and Don José and his men march in, followed by a swarm of street urchins.

"A charming girl was asking for you a few minutes ago," Morales tells José. "She had braids and wore a blue dress."

"Micaela!" exclaims the young man eagerly.

Captain Zuniga, in command of the new watch, questions José about the girls of the factory. As he talks, the noon-hour bell clangs and the square fills with workmen. The cigarette girls come out slowly, smoking and staring brazenly at the men. But where is Carmen?

There is a sudden stir and a dark-eyed gypsy darts into the square. She has a blood-red flower in her mouth. The men crowd about, crying, "Carmen, when will you be ours?" She looks at them mockingly. Then her glance falls on Don José, who sits quietly at one side mending a link in his chain.

"Not today, that is certain," she replies, and, her eyes on the young dragoon, she sings the haunting Habanera: "Love is like a wild woodbird. . . ."

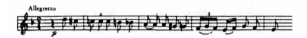

Joyously the crowd joins in. José pays not the slightest heed, and Carmen's eyes flash dangerously. "Love me not, and I will love you," she sings. "But then, beware!" She flings the red flower at him and runs away. Laughing, the mob disperses as the factory bell rings again. José is left alone.

He picks up the flower. "If there are witches in this world, she is surely one," he muses. Then, seeing Micaela approach, he quickly thrusts the blossom inside his jacket.

The two greet each other warmly. Micaela brings him a letter from his mother, also a kiss. . . . The young man is very much moved. "You bring back memories of home," he tells her.

The girl leaves him with his letter, promising to return, and he reads the message in silence. "Do not fear, Mother," he says softly. "I love Micaela and will marry her as you wish. As for your flowers, you sorceress. . . ."

From the factory come cries for help, and the girls rush out, arguing violently. A fight has taken place; Captain Zuniga sends José to investigate. A few minutes later the young man returns with Carmen, who has been fettered. But the girl refuses to answer the captain's questions. "Tra la-la-la," she sings impudently. "You may beat me, you may burn me. I won't tell a thing."

"Sing in jail then," Zuniga retorts, going into the guardhouse.

Alone with José, the gypsy tells him that the flower she threw at him was charmed. "You will release me. I know it," she declares, and, swinging her skirts brazenly, she sings of the pleasures of Lillas Pastia's tavern near the walls of Seville:

"There I will dance the gay seguidille, and drink manzanilla with my friend, an officer who loves me and knows that I will wait for him. . . ."

"Carmen," cries José in agitation. "Will you be faithful if I love you? Will you love me?"

"Yes," she murmurs.

He cuts the knot that binds her hands. Just then Zuniga comes out with the order for Carmen's arrest. José marches off with the gypsy. But as they cross the bridge at the back, the girl shoves her captor violently. He falls, and she escapes, laughing, down a back alley.

ACT TWO. Carmen and her friends, Frasquita and Mercedes, are sitting at a table in Lillas Pastia's inn with Captain Zuniga. Before them in the dim lamplight a crowd of gypsy maidens dance to the accompaniment of guitars and tambourines. Carmen sings a lilting song:

But it has grown late. Zuniga urges Carmen to come away with him. "Do not be vexed with me," he says. "The dragoon we put in jail for letting you escape is free again."

Outside. shouts are heard, and Escamillo swaggers in. He is followed by a crowd of admirers who drink his health, and in answer he launches into a description of bull-fighting:

As he sings, his eyes seek out Carmen. "What is your name?" he asks. "The next time I am in danger I will use it as a charm." She tells him.

"And supposing I say that I love you?"

"I would tell you that it is useless."

"Well, I will wait," he replies good-naturedly, and departs with Zuniga. At once two rough-looking men, the smugglers Dancaïro and Remendado, hasten out of an inner room. They urge the three girls to help them carry out a venture planned for that night.

"I cannot go," Carmen tells them. "I am in love."

They beg her to change her mind, but the voice of Don José outside cuts short their arguments. "Try to get him to join us," suggest the smugglers as they leave, and Carmen promises to try.

José rushes into the room. "What a joy it is to see you again," he cries ardently. Carmen picks up her castanets. Singing a haunting little melody. she dances about the young man. who watches her. fascinated. Suddenly a bugle sounds in the distance. José stops Carmen abruptly. "Wait a minute. They are playing retreat. I shall have to leave."

"Leave!" Carmen is stupified. Here she has been dancing and singing for him, she might even have loved him, and at the call of a bugle he is off. Furious, she flings his sabre and cap after him.

"Carmen. you must listen to me." he cries desperately. and. taking out the flower she threw at him so long ago, he tells her that it has been his companion through all the weary days of his imprisonment.

"I live only for you. I love you. Carmen."
"No, if you did you would follow me to the hills," she replies.

José hesitates. But to desert is infamy, and, bidding her farewell, he hastens toward the door. There is a knock.

Startled, José halts, and a minute later Zuniga forces in the door. He taunts Carmen for choosing a corporal when she might have a captain; then, turning to the young man, he orders him to his barracks.

"Never!" replies José, wild with jealousy. The two men draw their swords, but the gypsies rush in and separate them.

"Now will you come with us?" asks Carmen.

As a deserter, José has no choice but to join the outlaws.

THE THIRD ACT opens on a wild gorge in the mountains. Dancaïro and his men file in stealthily:

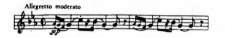

They are carrying bales of stolen goods which they set down while scouts are sent ahead to see if the way is clear. José stares down gloomily into the valley, thinking of his mother who still believes in him.

"Why don't you go back to her?" taunts Carmen.

"And leave you?" José fingers his knife. "Beware what you say."

Carmen laughs scornfully. "Perhaps you will kill me," she suggests.

Mercedes and Frasquita are telling their fortunes:

Carmen goes over to watch. For one the cards promise a poor but gallant lover; for the other, an old man with a fortune.

"Let me try my hand," cries Carmen. She deals out the cards. "Spades! Death! First for me and then for him!" She reshuffles the pack. "Again, Death!"

Dancaïro returns with the news that the road is clear except for three guards, whom the girls will engage in conversation while the others slip through. Don José is to guard the remaining goods. He takes up his position among the rocks and the smugglers depart.

Hardly have they left when Micaela comes forward out of the gloom. She looks about her fearfully. "Shall I find him here? I will carry out his mother's wishes, but O merciful Heaven, protect me. . . ."

She sees José on the rocks above, but instead of coming down he takes aim with his rifle. A shot rings out. Micaela hides in terror. At that moment a stalwart figure swings up through the pass, examining a bullet hole in his hat. "Who goes there?" challenges José.

"Escamillo. Toreador of Granada."

Climbing down, José greets the bull fighter warmly.

"I've come after my gypsy lass," Escamillo tells him. "Her name is Carmen, and the last I knew she was in love with a dragoon from Seville. But her love never lasts more than six months."

José draws his knife. "On guard," he warns. "I am he!"

The two men rush at each other savagely, dodging and slashing.

Escamillo's blade snaps. But as José is about to strike him Carmen seizes his arm from behind, and the incoming gypsies rush between the men.

"Thanks for your timely help," says Escamillo, bowing gallantly. "Now let me invite all of you to the bull fight at Seville. Anyone who loves me will come." He looks at Carmen, who returns his bold stare, then departs slowly.

The smugglers also make ready to leave. Micaela is discovered.

"What are you doing here?" gasps José, as the girl is dragged forward.

"Down there in her lonely cottage your mother is weeping for you," she replies. "Have pity on her, and return with me."

"Yes, go," Carmen urges.

"So that you can be free to follow your toreador?" cries José violently. "Never!"

"But your mother is dying," pleads Micaela.

Horrified, José agrees to go with her. He takes a few steps, then stops. "We will meet again, Carmen," he threatens, and hastens off.

From the distance comes the voice of Escamillo, singing the Toreador Song. Carmen listens exultantly. She will live for Escamillo, regardless of Fate.

ACT FOUR. A festive crowd fills the square in front of the arena at Seville. Peddlers offer their wares, street dancers in brilliant shawls whirl and glide to the music of Bizet's *l'Arlésienne* and *Pearlfisher Suites*, played in the orchestra. Then, led by a band, the procession to the arena begins. The city officials pass through the square, followed by row on row of bull fighters, the sunlight gleaming on their long lances.

Suddenly the crowd gives a wild shout. Escamillo, the favorite of the day, has arrived, and with him is Carmen, gorgeous in a spangled dress and fringed shawl.

He smiles down at her proudly. "Do you love me?"

"Yes," she whispers, flushing with excitement. The toreador enters the arena. As the people stream after him, Mercedes and Frasquita slip to Carmen's side. "You must not stay here," they warn her. "José is lurking in the crowd."

"I am not the woman to fear him," Carmen replies. "I shall wait here." Her friends rejoin the crowd, and they all enter the arena.

José steps from behind an archway. Haggard and despairing, he approaches Carmen, who awaits him defiantly. "I am told you intend to kill me."

Instead he implores her to forget all that has passed. "Carmen, I love you. Let us flee far from here and begin life over again." But she rejects him; all is finished between them. José starts violently. Finished! No, that cannot be. He will rejoin the smugglers' band, he will do whatever she asks.

From the arena rises a shout of triumph. Carmen tries to push past José.

"You shall not go in there, you are coming with me," he cries roughly.

"Let me go," she screams, wrenching away. "I love him."

A fanfare sounds. "Viva, toreador!" shout the people. "Remember the dark-eyed lady who waits for you."

Furious, José draws his dagger. Carmen tries to escape, but he catches up with her at the entrance and stabs her. She falls.

The people swarm back. "Do whatever you want with me," José cries hoarsely, and throws himself beside the body. "O, my Carmen, my beloved Carmen, you are gone."

José fingers his knife.

Cavalleria Rusticana

(RUSTIC CHIVALRY)

BY PIETRO MASCAGNI

Libretto by Targioni-Tozzetti and Menasci,
adapted from story by Giovanni Verga

PRINCIPAL CHARACTERS *(in order of appearance):*

Santuzza (soprano), a young peasant girl.
Mamma Lucia (contralto), the village innkeeper.
Alfio (baritone), a good-natured teamster.
Turridu (tenor), son of Mamma Lucia, recently returned from service in the army.
Lola (mezzo-soprano), the brazen young wife of Alfio.
PLACE: A village in Sicily.   TIME: The nineteenth century.

THE PRELUDE begins softly and fatefully, as if a day of tragedy were dawning. Then a pleading melody whispers of Santuzza's love:

Suddenly, Turiddu's voice is heard in the distance, singing: "O, Lola, your lips are like crimson berries. . . . There is blood on your doorstep, Lola. But what do I care, so long as I die with you?"

The orchestra bursts out passionately, then fades away, and a new melody sounds, describing Santuzza's longing and despair:

The curtain rises on the square before the church. It is Easter morning and the bells are tolling to call the people to worship. Gradually the square fills with villagers and country folk. Some go into the church, others gather to talk a bit before going on. When at last the square is empty again, Santuzza hurries over to the tavern opposite the church and knocks on the door. An old peasant woman comes out.

"Tell me where your son is hiding, Mamma Lucia," the girl pleads.

"He went to fetch wine from Francofonte."

"No! Last night he was seen in the village. . . ."

"Who told you that?" snaps the old woman uneasily. "I, his mother, haven't seen him. . . . But come inside."

"I cannot," Santuzza replies, shrinking back, "I am excommunicated."

The jingling of wagon bells sounds in the alley, and a minute later Alfio drives into the square. "My steed steps proudly, the bells ring gaily," sings the teamster, snapping his long whip.

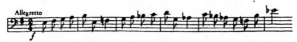

"Easter is the time to come home to my little Lola." A crowd of townsfolk have come in with him, and, laughing, they join in the chorus.

"Good morning, Mamma Lucia," Alfio calls cheerfully. "Have you still the same good wine as always?"

"Turiddu has gone to buy some in the next town," she replies.

Alfio scratches his head. "That's strange! I saw him near my house."

The old peasant looks up in surprise, but Santuzza signs to her to say nothing, and presently Alfio goes on his way.

Most of the people have gone into church. Now the organ peals out and the choir begins to sing an Easter anthem. "Hallelujah!" cry the people, and those still outside fall upon their knees. Santuzza sinks down with them, joining in the song of thanksgiving:

All but Santuzza and Mamma Lucia go into the church. "Why did you tell me to keep quiet when Alfio was here?" the old woman demands.

"You know that Turiddu plighted his troth to Lola before he went to war," Santuzza answers. "When he found her married to Alfio on his return, he tried to forget her by making love to me. . . ." Her voice breaks. "And I—I loved him with all my heart. . . . But Lola envied my happiness, and lured him away from me. Now she and Turiddu love each other again, and I am left alone to weep. . . .

"O. Mamma Lucia, pray that Heaven will pity me.".

Deeply moved, the old peasant goes into the church.

Turiddu swaggers across the square. "You here, Santuzza?" he asks lightly, trying to push past her. She bars his way.

"Turiddu, you were seen near Lola's house this morning."

He turns on her angrily. "So you have been spying on me?"

"No. Alfio saw you. O. Turiddu, don't you love me any more?"

Instead of answering her questions, he tells her roughly not to be so jealous. Santuzza bursts into tears.

At that moment, a wanton voice sounds in the alley. It is Lola. "My king of roses," she sings, "the angels cannot compare with you."

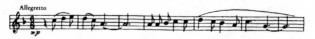

Turning the corner, she sees the others and stops abruptly. "I am looking for Alfio," she remarks carelessly. "Aren't you going to Mass?"

"Today is Easter," Santuzza says pointedly. "Only those should go who are free of sin."

"Well, I am going." declares Lola. and glances at Turiddu. "Why don't you stay with poor Santuzza?" Humming her flower song, she walks up the steps, but at the door she turns quickly and tosses a rose at her lover with a mocking smile. He snatches it up.

Wild with grief, Santuzza catches Turiddu by the arm, imploring him to stay. "Will you spy on me in church, too?" he shouts.

"Ah. how can you have the heart to forsake me?" she sobs.

Hurling her savagely to the ground, he bounds up the steps into the church. Santuzza sways to her knees. "Be accursed!" she shrieks after him. and sinks down, overcome with despair.

Steps ring on the cobblestones. Santuzza has barely time to get to her feet when Alfio enters. "Heaven itself must have sent you to me, Alfio." she cries, staring at the teamster with wild hard eyes. "Lola has gone to church with Turiddu!"

"What do you mean?" exclaims Alfio, startled.

Turiddu hurls her to the ground.

"I mean that while you were away Lola stole Turiddu from me!"

There is a long silence. "Thank you very much, Santuzza," says the teamster at last. Then suddenly he bursts out furiously. "They shall pay with their lives—before sunset," he rages, and rushes away.

Horrified, Santuzza gazes after him. She has betrayed her lover—perhaps to his death. In an agony of remorse, she runs after Alfio.

The sunlight shines down on the quiet, empty square. From the church comes the rich sound of the organ, but now a lovely melody—the famous *Intermezzo*—soars above it:

At last the service ends and the people stream into the street. Turiddu comes out with Lola. "Don't hurry off," he whispers to her, and invites

the villagers to have a drink with them at his mother's tavern. Raising
his glass, Turiddu sings a gay drinking song:

As he finishes, Alfio appears suddenly. "Greetings. neighbor," shout
the merrymakers, and Turiddu offers him a glass.

The teamster pushes it away. "Thanks, no. It might be poison!" A
hush falls over the company.

The women persuade Lola to go away with them.

When they have left Turiddu faces his rival. "I am at your service,"
he declares, and bites the teamster on the ear in the Sicilian manner
of challenging to a duel.

"Good! I accept your invitation," responds Alfio grimly. "I'll wait
behind the garden." He stalks away, and the crowd disperses silently.

Turiddu is left at the empty table. He leaps up and runs to the inn
door. "Mamma," he calls, his voice shrill with fear. "Mamma, I have
something to tell you." Lucia hurries out.

"Do you remember when I went away to be a soldier?' he asks.
"Mamma, give me your blessing now the way you did then . . . and
if I shouldn't return, promise that you'll take care of Santuzza. . . ."

"What are you talking about?" cries the old woman in fear.

"O, nothing," he answers wildly. "The wine has gone to my head.
Dearest Mamma, pray that God will forgive me, and give me a kiss—a
last kiss. . . ." He runs off in despair.

From beyond the square where he has disappeared comes the murmur of excited voices. Filled with dread, Lucia makes her way toward
the growing crowd. Santuzza rushes in and throws her arms about the
old peasant's neck. Together they wait, listening.

Then a woman's shriek rings out. One of the village girls comes
rushing toward them, her face white. "Turiddu is murdered!" she
screams. "Alfio has killed him!" With a shriek, Santuzza falls in front of
the church. The grim tragedy has come to an end.

Don Giovanni

BY WOLFGANG AMADEUS MOZART

Libretto by Lorenzo da Ponte

PRINCIPAL CHARACTERS (in order of appearance):

Leporello (bass), the servant of Don Giovanni.

Donna Anna (soprano), beautiful daughter of the Commandant of Seville. She is in love with Don Ottavio, a young nobleman.

Don Giovanni (baritone), a handsome, ruthless cavalier, who spends his time in revelry and countless love affairs.

The Commandant of Seville (bass), a haughty, impetuous old nobleman.

Don Ottavio (tenor), the fiancé of Donna Anna.

Donna Elvira (soprano), a noble lady of Burgos whom Don Giovanni has betrayed.

Zerlina (soprano), a flirtatious peasant girl.

Masetto (bass), her jealous bridegroom.

PLACE: Seville, in Spain.   TIME: The eighteenth century.

THE OVERTURE begins with ominous chords that thunder through the orchestra like avenging Fate:

Then the mood changes. Swift and flashing, the music seems to suggest the pleasure-seeking Don as he rushes recklessly from one adventure to another, with never a thought for the sorrow he leaves behind him.

ACT ONE, *Scene One.* The curtain rises on a courtyard in the palace of the Commandant of Seville. It is night. Half hidden in shadow, Leporello sits on a stone bench. "Here I wait," he complains, "keeping watch while my master pays court to yet another lady. And what do I get for my pains? Poor pay! Hard work!" He gets up indignantly. "Well, I won't do it any more. I'm far too talented for such drudgery. . . ."

At that moment Don Giovanni bursts from the palace followed by Donna Anna. Leporello slips discreetly out of sight. The girl clings to the Don's arm, trying frantically to snatch away the cloak that conceals his face. "I *will* find out who you are," she cries. Angrily Don Giovanni attempts to wrench himself away. Donna Anna screams for help.

Her cries are answered by the Commandant, who rushes from the palace, sword in hand. "Defend yourself," he shouts. Donna Anna hastens away for assistance, and, scarcely able to control his rage, the old man slashes at his opponent. Don Giovanni parries his blows easily. Then suddenly he thrusts. The Commandant falls.

As the murderer and his servant slip away, Donna Anna returns with Don Ottavio and a crowd of attendants. Their torches light up the courtyard, and in the wavering glow the girl sees her father stretched before her. With a shriek she flings herself on his body. Don Ottavio seeks to comfort her. Together they swear an oath of vengeance.

Scene Two. Far from repenting of his crime of the night before, Don Giovanni hastens along a street with Leporello, bound for a fresh adventure. Suddenly he stops. The breeze has brought a whiff of perfume. "A woman!" he cries joyfully, and hastily drags his companion out of sight.

A heavily veiled lady enters. "How can I forget my dear one's tenderness?" she laments, pacing up and down in agitation.

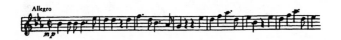

"Yet his treachery shattered all my dreams. Ah, wretch, you shall see how a woman can avenge herself."

"She has been betrayed, that is clear," remarks Giovanni mockingly to Leporello. "Well. I will comfort her." He steps forward and doffs his hat gallantly. "Madame."

Turning, the lady flings up her veil. It is Donna Elvira. one of his past loves. Don Giovanni is horrified, and looks about for some way to escape. But she confronts him with flashing eyes. "So, I have found you! Perhaps you will explain why you deserted me in Burgos?"

"Ask this honest fellow here." he replies, hauling Leporello from his hiding place. "Tell her the whole truth, knave."

"Yes, do," she urges. Don Giovanni slips away around the corner.

Leporello sees that he cannot escape too, so, drawing a book from his pocket, he assumes an air of importance. "Madame," says he, "you are neither the first nor the last to be fooled by that worthless fellow. See here." and he shows her the contents of his book—an enormous list of names, all victims of Don Giovanni.

"Italy boasts six hundred and forty," he goes on, "Germany two hundred and thirty-one, France a hundred. Turkey a trifling ninety-one, and Spain one thousand and three." He opens the book like a map. "Some, you see, are peasant lassies, some ladies of breeding. But tall or short, fat or slim, my master loves to flirt with them all." He folds up the list with a mocking smile, sticks it in his pocket, and runs off.

Donna Elvira is furious. "I will have revenge," she cries.

Scene Three. A crowd of peasants is making merry in a meadow on the outskirts of Seville in honor of the coming wedding of pretty Zerlina and her peasant bridegroom. Masetto. Into this scene of gaiety bursts Don Giovanni, followed by his knavish servant.

"Are we rid of Elvira at last?" he gasps.

His eye falls on Zerlina. Sweeping off his hat. he asks her name.

"Zerlina," she replies. "And this is my bridegroom, Masetto." The peasant makes an awkward bow.

"I am glad to meet you," declares the Don jovially. "Leporello, take these good people up to my palace and show them about. . . . Particularly Masetto," he adds in a whisper. Leporello nods.

"Let us be off," he cries, pushing between Masetto and Zerlina. But the peasant is unwilling to go without his bride, and it is only after Don Giovanni fingers his sword that he stumbles after the others angrily.

At once Don Giovanni slips his arm around the girl's waist. "You are far too lovely for Masetto," he declares. "I will marry you."

"You?" she exclaims in astonishment.

"Why not? Give me your hand, my darling, and whisper 'yes.' "

The girl is very much flattered, but hesitates, thinking of Masetto.

Donna Elvira enters hastily. "So you are planning to deceive this poor child, too," she cries indignantly, and, snatching the girl from the angry nobleman, she hurries her into a near-by tavern.

For once Don Giovanni is baffled. He turns to go, then suddenly notices Donna Anna and Ottavio making their way across the meadow. It is too late to escape. They greet him courteously, and Donna Anna begs him to help her. Don Giovanni breathes a sigh of relief. So they have not yet recognized him as the Commandant's assassin.

"My sword is at your service," he assures them.

At that moment Elvira rushes from the tavern. "Do not trust him," she cries wildly. "He is an arch-criminal, a fiend."

Donna Anna and Ottavio are amazed.

"Pay no attention; she is mad," explains Don Giovanni, and suggests that the others leave her to him. Elvira begs them to stay. The Don fears that they will discover his secret, and tries in vain to silence her. At last he succeeds in leading her away. Donna Anna stares after him in horror.

"Ottavio, that is the murderer of my father," she half screams. "Those tones, those gestures! O, there is no doubt."

Reminding him of his oath, she implores the young man to avenge the Commandant's death. He nods assent. Donna Anna goes off; and, left alone, Ottavio vows to bring his foe to justice.

Scene Four. Don Giovanni's difficulties with Zerlina have not discouraged him. Meeting Leporello on the terrace of his palace, he bids him prepare a feast for the peasants. "Let us have fountains of wine," he cries gaily, "and music to set the maidens dancing."

The two go inside.

Masetto enters the garden, followed by Zerlina. "Dearest, just let me explain," she pleads. But the peasant is in a huff and will not listen. She puts her arms about his neck. "Beat me, darling Masetto, if you think I deserve it," she begs, "only love me again."

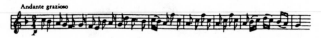

He is just about to relent when they hear the voice of Don Giovanni within. Zerlina turns pale. "What shall we do?" she cries.

"You are afraid I will discover your secrets!" replies Masetto angrily. "Well, I will hide in this summerhouse, so be careful what you say, Miss." He slips inside an arbor.

It has become quite dark, and now the peasants arrive for the feast. Don Giovanni greets them on the steps, looking everywhere for Zerlina. The girl has hidden behind some bushes, but he soon discovers her, and, paying no heed to her protests, draws her toward the arbor. Out steps Masetto.

"Masetto!" exclaims the astonished nobleman. "Why, we were just looking for you," he adds quickly, and leads them both into the palace.

Hardly have they left when three masked figures appear on the terrace. Elvira has joined forces with Donna Anna and Ottavio, and the three have come to seek out the murderer. Leporello, who has sauntered to the balcony for a breath of air, takes them for revelers.

"You are welcome to the ball," he calls cheerfully.

The strangers bow. "Heaven grant us vengeance," they murmur, and go into the palace.

Scene Five. Within, all is merriment. In various parts of the hall three orchestras are playing, one a lilting minuet:

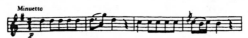

another a gavotte, the third a swaying waltz. The host dances a minuet with Zerlina, gradually leading her toward a secret alcove, while Leporello tries to distract Masetto's attention in the next room. In the background the three conspirators bide their time.

At last Don Giovanni reaches the alcove. Wrenching open the door, he forces the screaming girl inside. At once the place is in an uproar. Masetto and the peasants dash in the alcove door, and Zerlina rushes out to her bridegroom's arms.

Leporello hastens to warn his master of his peril but, whipping out his sword, the Don forces his servant to his knees.

"You would offend the girl, would you?" he shouts, pretending that Leoporello had done the mischief.

His trick fails. Donna Anna and her friends tear off their masks and face him indignantly. For a moment Don Giovanni does not know which way to turn. Then, beating down Don Ottavio's sword, he slashes through the mob of peasants and escapes into the night.

ACT TWO. *Scene One*. Sad and lonely, Donna Elvira paces the square before her house, thinking of Don Giovanni. "His crimes will surely bring him to judgment," she reflects. "And yet I love him still. . . . Is there no way that I can aid him?"

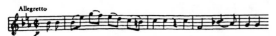

The sound of approaching footsteps rings through the quiet street, and she goes within. A pale moon has risen above the housetops. Here and there lights glimmer in the twilight.

"Well, Sir Stupid," cries a familiar voice. "What is your complaint now?" Wrapped in a cloak and carrying a mandolin, Don Giovanni enters the square, followed by Leporello, who is very much out of humor.

"I am leaving your service," he insists. "You tried to kill me."

The Don laughs and slips him a purse. "That was only a joke."

"Very well," replies the knave. "But leave the women alone."

Don Giovanni stares at him in astonishment. Why, he would rather flirt with a pretty girl than eat!

"Have you seen Elvira's delightful servant maid?" he asks Leporello. "I am about to visit her, and want to borrow your cloak and hat."

As they exchange clothing, Donna Elvira comes out on the balcony above. Quickly Don Giovanni pushes his servant forward. "You make love to her," he whispers. Then, concealing himself, he begs Elvira to come down. "I have wronged you," he cries. "O, my dearest, let me beg your forgiveness."

Elvira starts as she hears Don Giovanni's voice. She looks over the balcony. Surely that is he, standing below her in the shadows. Wild with joy, she hastens down to the waiting arms of Leporello. Cleverly concealing his face, the knave protests his love, until, startled by a sudden noise, the two run off. The square is empty.

At once Don Giovanni comes forward, busily tuning his mandolin. "Fairest maiden, let your radiance shine on me," he sings, gazing up in the hope of seeing Elvira's maid.

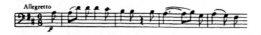

Suddenly a crowd of men push into the dark square. "There is someone by that window," calls a voice. "Answer or we will fire." Don Giovanni recognizes Masetto.

"I am Leporello," he replies, pulling his hat over his eyes.

The peasants tell him that they are looking for Don Giovanni. Does he know where the scoundrel is hiding?

"Why, yes," answers the Don; and, giving them false directions, he scatters them throughout the city. Masetto remains behind to discuss a plan of action.

"Have you good weapons?" Don Giovanni asks him.

Quite unsuspecting, the peasant hands him his musket, bludgeon, and pistol. A minute later he finds himself on the ground.

"*That* for your fine intentions," shouts Don Giovanni, beating him unmercifully. Then, snatching up his mandolin, he slips off.

Half-dead with fright, Masetto huddles on the ground, groaning.

Zerlina runs into the square. "What has happened?" she cries.

"That villain, Leporello, has broken every bone in my body," he moans.

Zerlina embraces him tenderly. "Come home with me, you foolish fellow. I will cure you. But next time don't be so jealous."

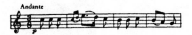

Scene Two. Still pretending that he is Don Giovanni, Leporello flees with Elvira into a courtyard of the Commandant's palace. He has grown tired of her words of love, and gropes about in the dark for a way of escape. His hand falls on a door knob. As he tugs at it, the door suddenly opens inward. Donna Anna comes out, followed by Ottavio and attendants with torches. The girl is weeping bitterly, still overcome by her father's death, and Ottavio tries to comfort her.

Meanwhile Leporello has noticed a door on the far side of the court. He creeps toward it cautiously. But Elvira has also seen the door.

"Does that wretch plan to desert me again?" she wonders, looking about for her supposed lover. Slipping out of the nook in which she has hidden, she also makes her way toward the door. It opens with a crash.

In rush Masetto and Zerlina and pounce on Leporello. Terrified, he tears away his disguise. "I am Leporello," he howls. "Spare me."

Zerlina turns on him angrily. "So it was you who beat my poor Masetto," she cries. Donna Elvira is furious at finding that she has been deceived again, and Masetto, remembering his bruises, shakes his stick threateningly.

"I am innocent of all this mischief," protests Leporello, edging toward the door. "My master, Don Giovanni, is to blame." Suddenly he ducks past those nearest him, and is off down the lane as fast as his legs can carry him.

The peasants follow in pursuit, and, as the ladies withdraw, Ottavio again vows to bring Don Giovanni to justice. "Then, beloved Anna, you will have peace," he promises.

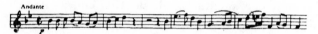

Scene Three. Fleeing from the townsfolk, Don Giovanni and Lepo-

"Madame, you are neither the first nor the last to be fooled by Don Giovanni."

rello meet in a graveyard. The Don is in high spirits, and gaily relates his latest adventure. Suddenly a hollow voice echoes through the night: "Your mirth will turn to woe before morning."

Startled, Don Giovanni wheels. "Who spoke?"

Behind him, in the dim moonlight, he sees a huge marble statue of a man on horseback. It is the monument of the murdered Commandant. "Read the inscription," he commands Leporello.

Trembling with fright, the valet approaches the statue. "Here I await the vengeance decreed by Heaven on him who slew me," he reads falteringly. Don Giovanni laughs.

"Good," he cries. "Invite his lordship to dinner this very evening."

Leporello shrinks in terror. "I dare not," he screams, pointing at the statue. "He is alive. See how he glares at you."

Don Giovanni thrusts the grovelling wretch to one side. "Will you come to supper?" he asks the statue defiantly. "Answer, if you are able." There is a moment of awful silence. Then the stone figure seems to bow its head in assent. "Yes," thunders a fearful voice.

Dragging his servant after him, the Don goes off to prepare the feast.

Scene Four. In the vestibule outside Donna Anna's apartment, Don Ottavio is trying to sooth the grief of his fiancée. "We shall soon have vengeance," he promises, and he implores her to marry him—to forget her sorrow in joy. Donna Anna draws back.

"You are cruel to delay our happiness," he cries reproachfully.

"Ah, no, do not say that, Ottavio," she answers. "Your grief saddens my heart, but still we must wait until my father has been avenged."

Scene Five. Don Giovanni is feasting in his palace. The hall is aglitter with the light of hundreds of candles, and on the balcony at one side a band of musicians plays familiar melodies. Leporello divides his time between serving his master and slyly sampling the dainties that load down the sideboard. Suddenly the door is thrown open.

Donna Elvira rushes wildly into the room and flings herself on her knees before Don Giovanni. "Danger threatens you," she cries. "O repent, I beg you, before it is too late." The Don laughs cheerfully.

"Long live the ladies. They are the glory of the earth," he cries, and invites her to sup with him. Furious, Elvira turns to go. But at the door she starts back with a shriek of horror.

Don Giovanni and Leporello stare at each other in astonishment. "Go see what is the matter," orders the Don. Leporello seizes a candlestick and hastens to the door.

"Ahhhh!" he screams.

"Well, what is it?" shouts Don Giovanni, shaking him.

"The huge white man, the statue," chatters Leporello. "Ta! Ta! Ta! Ta! he comes striding. . . . Listen!" he shrieks.

A loud knock is heard.

"Open the door," commands Don Giovanni, threatening the terror-stricken servant with his sword. But Leporello is powerless to move. Springing forward himself, the Don flings wide the great doors of the palace.

On the threshold stands the colossal stone statue of the Commandant.

"Don Giovanni, I have come to your banquet," says the awful voice.

Trying to bolster his courage, the Don orders Leporello to spread the table. But the statue interrupts. Instead he proposes that Don Giovanni feast with him, and asks for his hand as a pledge.

"Here it is," cries the nobleman defiantly; but, as the marble fingers close on his, wild terror seizes him at last.

"Repent of your evil ways," thunders the phantom.

"No!" shrieks the Don, struggling to free himself.

"Then go to your doom!" With a crash the statue sinks through the floor. Flames leap up. Frantically Don Giovanni tries to escape, but he is hemmed in on every side. With a cry of despair he sinks into the abyss.

Epilogue. Crouching under a table, Leporello has seen the terrible fate of his master, and now he scurries off to tell his tale. Donna Anna, Elvira, Don Ottavio, and the peasant couple, Zerlina and Masetto, listen, awe-struck. Then, advancing to the footlights, they warn the audience that a similar fate awaits all scoundrels.

Faust

BY CHARLES-FRANÇOIS GOUNOD

Libretto, based on Goethe's drama (much altered), by Barbier and Carré

PRINCIPAL CHARACTERS *(in order of appearance):*

Faust (tenor), an aged philosopher, who has spent a lifetime vainly seeking to solve the mystery of the universe.

Mephistopheles (bass-baritone), who is Satan in human shape.

Valentin (baritone), a young soldier.

Siebel (mezzo-soprano), a youth in love with Valentin's sister, Marguerite.

Marguerite (soprano).

Martha (contralto), a middle-aged lady with whom Valentin leaves his sister while he is away at the wars.

PLACE: The town of Nuremberg, Germany.   TIME: The sixteenth century.

PRELUDE: Mysterious harmonies create an atmosphere of melancholy. A lovely melody steals briefly through the orchestra:

Then the sombre chords return and the curtain rises on a gloomy vaulted chamber.

ACT ONE, *Scene One*. At a massive table, heaped high with books and parchments, sits Faust, bending over an ancient volume. A flickering lamp lights his work and casts grotesque shadows on the walls.

Dawn is breaking, and pale light shines through the dusty panes of the window.

"Another weary day," cries the old man. "Why should I not seek the release of death? I am the master of my own destiny." Rising, he hastily empties the contents of a vial into a goblet, and raises it to his lips.

The sound of voices stops him. Beyond, in the fields, peasant girls and laborers sing of the beauty of nature and the joys of love.

"Praise be to God!" they cry.

Faust dashes his goblet to the floor. "Away, vain echoes!" he screams. "This God will never bring *me* youth and love and faith." He tears his long gray locks in a frenzy of despair. "Curses on all this vile human race. Come to me, Satan, come to me!"

"I am here," thunders a voice behind him in the shadows. Faust turns quickly. There stands a sinister figure, clad in eerie green and red.

"Well!" cries Mephistopheles. "What will you have, my friend?"

"Begone," mutters Faust fearfully.

The Devil will not go. "I can give you wealth, glory, power," he promises.

"I do not wish those things," answers the old man passionately. "I want youth—youth with its pleasures, its loves, its mad adventures."

Then he grows worried. "What must I give you in return?" he asks.

"O, very little," replies Mephistopheles. "Here I will serve you. Below, you must serve me."

Still Faust hesitates to sign away his soul.

"Look," shouts the Devil, and before the old man's eyes appears a vision of a young girl. Marguerite, seated at her spinning wheel.

Faust waits no longer. "To you, loveliest of maidens," he quavers, drinking at one draught the smoking potion that Mephistopheles offers him.

In an instant he is transformed. Where the old scholar had been stands a handsome youth, richly clad in doublet and hose, with a sword clanking at his hip. "Come, let us find her," he shouts exuberantly, and, with the Fiend at his heels, bursts through the door of his gloomy study out into the world.

Scene Two. Sunlight streams over the fair grounds outside one of the city gates. Students and soldiers are gathered at an inn, which has a little cask surmounted by an effigy of the wine god, Bacchus, over its doorway in place of a sign. The students are in the midst of a drinking bout, led by a young man named Wagner; the soldiers, who are about to depart for the war, join in boisterously. Over against the town wall sits a group of burghers, drinking at their ease. Then the square fills with young girls. They flirt with the students, much to the annoyance of the older women, who watch with envy.

Into this scene of gaiety comes Valentin, gazing sadly at a silver medallion. It was given to him by his sister, Marguerite, whom he is obliged to leave unprotected while he goes to war.

"I will watch over her," volunteers Siebel.

Valentin thanks him. "If I am spared in combat I will reward your fidelity," he declares, and the lovely melody heard in the prelude sounds again.

"Come now, friends," interrupts Wagner. "No vain tears. Let's drink to our success at arms," and he launches into a gay drinking song. "A rat more cowardly than brave lived in an old hohgshead. A cat. . ."

"Pardon!" cries a voice abruptly. In their midst stands a tall stranger, dressed in eerie green. "I know a better song," he declares.

Drawn by a curious fascination, the crowd gathers closely about as the newcomer mounts a table. "Calf of Gold, mighty god," he sings.

"All the world dances at your altar. Kings and peoples everywhere dance to the sound of clinking gold." He flings handfuls of coins into the air. The crowd scrambles about at his feet after them. "And Satan conducts the ball," he finishes, mockingly. "Satan conducts the ball," echoes the mob with enthusiasm.

Wagner offers the stranger a drink. "Ah," cries the latter. seizing Wagner's hand. "See this line on your palm, friend? You will perish in the coming battle."

"Sorcerer!" accuses Siebel.

The stranger turns to the youth quickly.

"The flowers you pluck will fade in your hand," he prophesies. "No more bouquets for Marguerite."

"How do you know my sister's name?" shouts Valentin in surprise.

"Take care, my brave fellow," replies the stranger. "You are destined to be killed by someone I know." He tastes the wine in his cup. "Pah! What miserable stuff!" Then, leaping upon the table, he strikes the little cask over the door. "Hither, Bacchus," he cries. Wine gushes out, filling his cup. He raises it ironically. "To Marguerite!"

Enraged, Valentin draws his sword. But the stranger quickly marks a circle about himself with his own weapon, and as the soldier lunges forward his sword breaks in mid air. Can this be the Devil himself?

"Why do you hesitate?" jeers Mephistopheles.

Valentin and the others lift the cross-shaped hilts of their swords, and as the Devil cringes before this holy sign they make their escape.

Faust appears, followed by youths and maidens who begin to dance gaily to the music of the town musicians. Presently Marguerite makes her way through the crowd. "There is the maiden of your choice," the Fiend whispers to Faust. "Go offer to escort her home."

But Marguerite rebuffs the young man's advances and continues on her way alone.

"What grace, what beauty," cries Faust, looking after her ardently. Then, accompanied by Mephistopheles, he pushes through the dancing students to follow Marguerite.

THE SECOND ACT opens in Marguerite's garden. Siebel enters through a little gate in the wall at the rear. "O lovely flowers, whisper to her of my love," he cries, stooping to pick some lilies and roses that grow at one end of the garden.

"Ah . . . they wither! Can the words of that accursed sorcerer be true?" He dips his fingers in a little vessel of holy water suspended from the wall. "Now I'll try again." He picks a few blossoms. This time they do not fade. "Satan, you are conquered," he cries triumphantly, and, as Faust and Mephistopheles steal in unseen by the gate at the rear, he makes a bouquet and lays it on the doorstep of the pavilion.

When the youth has gone, the Devil tells Faust that he will fetch him a present for Marguerite that will outshine all flowers. "Await me here," he cries, slipping away.

Left alone, the young man gazes up at the window. "O home of my beloved," he exclaims, "how beautiful you are."

Mephistopheles returns with a casket under his arm. "If flowers are more potent than jewels," he declares, showing Faust the contents of the box, "then I will release you from our bargain." He lays the casket under the bouquet, and the two hide in the shrubbery to watch.

Presently the gate opens and Marguerite enters.

"If only I knew the name of the youth who spoke to me today," she laments.

Her spinning wheel is in the arbor, and, as she arranges the flax on the spindle, she sings a mournful song: "Once there was a king of Thulé, who was faithful even until death. . . ."

Finally she rises with a sigh. "Ah, me, I won't think about the young man any more. If Heaven hears my prayers, we will meet again."

Suddenly she sees the bouquet on the doorstep. "Flowers! From my poor Siebel, without a doubt. . . . But what is this? A casket! And here

*Faust offers to
escort Marguerite home.*

is the key." She looks inside, then gives a little scream of delight. There is a mirror in the box and joyously she starts to deck herself in the glittering gems.

"Tell me, truly, can it be Marguerite?" she laughs, looking in the mirror.

"No, no, that bright face must belong to some queen. O, if only the young man might see me now he would surely take me for a fine lady."

At that moment Dame Martha enters. "Merciful Heaven! What is all this?" she exclaims. Marguerite is covered with confusion. She fears the jewels have been left there by mistake.

Then Mephistopheles steps out of hiding. "Dame Martha Schwerlein?" he inquires politely. Then, assuming an air of gravity, he informs her of her husband's death. But Martha is more interested in the handsome stranger than in his tragic news, and they wander off through the garden to talk.

Meanwhile Faust approaches Marguerite, who tries to send him away. At last, however, he captures her confidence, and she tells him of her loneliness. Faust responds ardently: "I love you, Marguerite." She flees into the garden. He follows, and Mephistopheles, who has finally rid himself of Martha, invokes the dark shades of approaching night and the magic fragrance of the flowers to help Faust conquer the heart of Marguerite. Then, as the lovers return, he slips off.

The moon has risen, shedding pale golden light over the garden. Faust implores Marguerite to linger with him, but, suddenly fearful, she tears herself from his arms and begs him to leave. "Till morning, my dearest," he agrees reluctantly, and she runs into the house.

"Fool!" cries Mephistopheles behind him in the darkness.

At that moment Marguerite opens her window in the upper floor of the building. "He loves me!" she cries, gazing out into the beautiful night. "Come back quickly, my beloved. O, if tomorrow were only here." Faust rushes to the house.

"Marguerite," he calls wildly, and as he climbs up the lattice to her window Mephistopheles goes out the garden gate, laughing triumphantly.

THE THIRD ACT, *Scene One,* opens on the dim interior of a church. Women enter silently, light tapers before a little shrine, and go into the pews beyond. Presently Marguerite crosses to the shrine. Faust has deserted her, and she has come to pray for forgiveness. As she prostrates herself, the voice of Mephistopheles rises as though from beneath her feet, forbidding her to pray.

The church choir begins a chant of worship, but the voice of the Fiend thunders in Marguerite's ears: "Remember the days when you came here with an unstained heart. Now you are doomed."

Terrified, she turns to look for her accuser. Suddenly the tomb near her opens and Mephistopheles stands before her, black and threatening. With a piercing scream Marguerite falls senseless to the ground. As the women in the pews run to help her, the apparition fades.

Scene Two. From the distance comes the rhythmic swing of a military marching song:

The curtain rises on a public square in Nuremberg. Girls are decking the houses with wreaths and flowers in honor of the re-turning troops. Hark! Here they come!

Marguerite awaits her execution.

The crowd rushes to the head of the street in excitement, then draws back to make room for the soldiers, who march down the lane, vivid in their scarlet uniforms and quaint flat caps. "Glory to those who have fallen in battle, glory to our native land," they exult.

Presently the square empties. Valentin remains.

"Siebel," exclaims Valentin, embracing the boy, who has been lingering near the house of Marguerite. The soldier turns eagerly to his home.

"Don't go in," begs Siebel, fearfully.

"What do you mean?" replies Valentin. Suddenly apprehensive, he hastens inside. Siebel goes toward the church as Faust and Mephistopheles come down the lane. The young man is regretful of the sorrow he has caused Marguerite, but his companion jeers at him. The Devil has a guitar, and now, advancing to Marguerite's window, he sings a mocking song that ends in a burst of coarse laughter.

Valentin rushes from the house. Furiously he shatters Mephistopheles' guitar.

Then he turns to Faust and challenges him to a duel.

"I will protect you," the Devil whispers to Faust; as Valentin lunges he strikes up his sword. Faust leaps forward and his sword pierces Valentin's breast. The soldier falls.

"Come, we must flee," cries Mephistopheles. The two depart hastily as the townsfolk, attracted by the noise of the fight, appear on the scene. "Valentin, Valentin," cries Marguerite, kneeling at his side. But he repulses her violently.

"Away!" he shouts. "Fool that I am, I die trying to punish the man who betrayed you. Be forever accursed!"

The crowd shrinks back in horror.

Valentin staggers to his feet. "I am a soldier," he cries, drawing himself erect. "Let me die like one." He falls at Marguerite's feet. With a cry of despair she throws herself on his body.

"God pardon his sins," murmur the people, kneeling.

ACT FOUR opens in a gloomy prison cell. Marguerite has gone mad and killed the child she bore to Faust. Now she awaits her execution. Suddenly the gate turns, clanking, on its rusty hinge, and the light of a lantern glimmers in the darkness. Faust has come to save Marguerite.

"Hasten," whispers Mephistopheles. "Day is dawning and we must be off. I will wait outside." Left alone, the young man gazes in horror at the wasted creature lying asleep on the pallet. "O, Marguerite," he cries, "what have I done to you?"

She wakes at the sound of his voice. "Is that you, my love?" she whispers. "Ah, now I am free, now I am saved." Her mind is wandering, and she imagines herself in the meadow outside the town where they first met, then in her garden where they spent so many happy hours. Faust is in despair.

"Hasten," calls Mephistopheles from the doorway. Marguerite starts back. "The Fiend," she gasps, and falling on her knees implores the aid of Heaven:

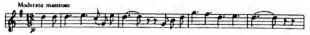

"We must leave," shouts Mephistopheles, trying to drag Faust along. "The fiery chargers are waiting." Faust tears himself out of the Devil's grasp.

"Come with me, Marguerite, my beloved," he begs.

"Is that blood on your hands?" she answers, rising and retreating before him in horror. "Begone! Begone, I say. I hate you." She falls dead.

"Condemned!" shrieks the Fiend in triumph.

But as he leaps forward to seize his victim, celestial voices stop him: "No. She is redeemed."

The prison fills with smoke. Through the blinding fumes, Mephistopheles drags Faust down into the depths that open before him.

Then the air clears and a vision of Marguerite appears, borne to heaven by winged angels. The curtain falls.

Fidelio

BY LUDWIG VAN BEETHOVEN

Libretto—a German version, by Sonnleithner,
of the French text by Bouilly
(later revised by Treitschke)

PRINCIPAL CHARACTERS *(in order of appearance):*

Jacquino (tenor), a turnkey at the state prison. He is in love with Marzelline.

Marzelline (soprano), the young daughter of the jailor.

Rocco (bass), her father, a good-hearted but avaricious old man.

Fidelio (soprano), the jailor's assistant, in reality Leonore Florestan, a lady of Seville, who appeared six months before disguised as a man and obtained work at the prison.

Don Pizarro (baritone), unscrupulous governor of the prison.

Florestan (tenor), Leonore's husband, a fearless and valiant enemy of the tyrant, Don Pizarro. Two years before Florestan had disappeared mysteriously.

Don Fernando (bass), Minister of Justice, and friend of Florestan.

PLACE: The Spanish state prison near Seville.   TIME: The eighteenth century.

ACT ONE, *Scene One*. After a brilliant overture, the curtain rises on a room in the gatehouse of the prison. Jacquino hovers about Marzelline, who is busy ironing. "Now we are alone and can talk," he begins eagerly. But the girl has no time to chatter with him.

"Why not?" he asks. "Marzelline, I have chosen a wife, and you know it is yourself." There is a knock at the door, and he runs off to answer it.

Marzelline looks after him pityingly. Ever since Fidelio came to work at the prison, she has been unable to think of anyone but the handsome stranger. "I think he is fond of me, too," she reflects. "O, how happy I would be if he asked me to be his wife."

Rocco comes into the room. "Hasn't Fidelio returned yet?" he asks uneasily. Even as he speaks the door opens, and Fidelio enters, laden down with provisions. "This time you have really burdened yourself too much," Rocco exclaims. "But never mind, my lad, you will have your reward."

"Please don't think I do my duty for the sake of reward," cries the supposed youth in confusion.

Marzelline is sure Fidelio loves her. "I am so happy," she whispers.

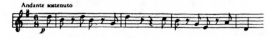

Fidelio, realizing that her own silence has been mistaken for love, wonders sadly how she can get out of this predicament.

The old jailor notices his daughter's ardent glances. Delighted at the idea of having such an industrious son-in-law, he declares that he will give Marzelline to Fidelio. "Be sure you have gold as well as love, though," he adds. "No marriage is happy without it."

"That is true," agrees Fidelio, "but there is something equally precious that I have never been able to win. And that is your confidence, Father Rocco. You never let me assist you with the prisoners."

"Yes, Fidelio should help you, Father," cries Marzelline. "You are killing yourself with overwork."

Much moved. the old man consents to ask the governor's permission to take his assistant with him on his rounds—although of course he would not be able to take him into the dungeon in which the mysterious prisoner has been confined for the last two years.

Two years! Fidelio starts violently.

Marzelline has noticed the supposed youth's deep emotion, and now she begs her father not to let his aide go with him.

"Why not?" interrupts Fidelio hastily. "I am not afraid."

"Good," answers Rocco.

At that moment. a military march is heard outside. The governor has arrived, and, taking the letters brought by Fidelio, Rocco hurries off.

Scene Two. Outside in the prison courtyard. a detachment of soldiers springs to attention as Pizarro strides through the gateway. "Post a double watch," he instructs the captain curtly. "Rocco, where are the dispatches?" The old man hands them to him.

Pizarro glances through the papers hastily. "Nothing but orders and reprimands," he mutters angrily. "But what is this? . . . 'The Minister of Justice suspects that you have victims of your own quarrels in the state dungeons, and will surprise you with a visit tomorrow.'" He crumples the letter furiously. "Supposing he should discover Florestan? . . . No! The hour of vengeance has come at last. and I will strike. . . .

Captain!" The man hastens forward, trembling.

"Take a trumpeter up into the tower and watch the road to Seville. The instant you see a carriage approaching, sound a warning." The soldiers march off.

Pizarro turns to Rocco. "I have work for you, old man." He throws a purse to the jailor, who seizes it eagerly.

"How can I serve you, sir?"

"Murder!"

Rocco drops the purse in horror. "Murder," he gasps. "No. your honor, my duty does not bind me to kill."

"Very well," answers Pizarro, enraged. "I will do it myself. But now go down to the prisoner in the deepest dungeon—you know the man —and dig a grave for him in the ruined well. When all is ready. give a signal; I will come down." He strides off, followed by Rocco.

As they disappear, Fidelio bursts from the house. "Monster! Demon in human shape!" she cries after Pizarro, her eyes flashing with anger. "Can no human misery move your savage soul to pity? . . .

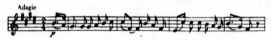

But still I will not give up hope. I am armed by the might of love, and Heaven will help me. . . . O, my dearest, for whom I dare everything, if only I might free you from your cruel bondage." She goes into the garden.

Marzelline and Jacquino enter, quarreling angrily. They meet Rocco, and the girl runs to him. "Jacquino is teasing me to marry him," she complains. The jailor shakes his head.

"I have other plans for her," he tells the young man.

Fidelio has returned. and now she approaches Rocco with the suggestion that they let the prisoners walk about for a while in the sunshine. The old man hesitates. Pizarro's discipline is strict, but, as he is about to do him a favor. he decides to risk the governor's anger. "Open only the minor cells," he cautions his assistants. "I will go and talk to Pizarro."

Fidelio and Jacquino unlock the prison doors. One by one, then in groups, a swarm of wasted creatures totter out of the dark fortress. "O golden sunshine," they murmur, shielding their eyes from the bright daylight. "O Freedom. when shall you be ours again?"

As they wander into the garden, Rocco returns. "The governor has agreed to let you help me," he tells Fidelio. "This very day we must go down to dig a grave for that poor man in the lowest dungeon. He will soon be dead."

"Is murder part of your work, then?" gasps the supposed youth.

"No. Pizarro himself will do the deed."

They are interrupted by Marzelline, who runs up, breathless. "The governor is coming," she stammers. "The guard told him that you let the prisoners out." As she speaks, Pizarro enters.

"How dare you take it upon yourself to release the prisoners?" he asks the jailor furiously. Rocco tries to appease him. The man in the lower dungeon is to die, so why not give the others a little joy?

"Very well," mutters the governor. "But never disobey again."

Jacquino and Fidelio herd the prisoners back into their cells. Then, shouldering their pickaxes, the jailor and his assistant go into the prison.

ACT TWO. *Scene One.* Empty chords echo through the orchestra, suggesting solitude and despair; the woodwinds wail out as though in pain. Then the curtain rises on a dungeon deep down under the fortress. In the gloom a man stirs feebly. "What darkness!" he cries. "What endless silence!" It is Florestan.

For two long years he has been chained to the rocky floor of his prison, alone with his thoughts. He stares off into space. "All the joy of life is gone forever," he reflects moodily.

"I fought for truth and right, and this is my reward." His voice rises feverishly. "Well, then, I will die for my duty. . . ."

Suddenly, he imagines that he sees his Leonore, come to lead him to the freedom of death. Exhausted, he sinks down unconscious.

The grate above creaks open. Fidelio and Rocco come slowly down the stairs. "Here is the well," whispers the jailor, going over to a heap of rocks and rubbish at one side. They set to work.

Presently Florestan raises his head. Rocco goes over to him.

"You are always deaf to my complaints," Florestan says weakly. "But at least tell me who is the governor of this prison."

"Don Pizarro."

"Pizarro!" cries the prisoner. "O, I pray you, send to Seville and ask for Leonore Florestan. . . ." The old man shakes his head sorrowfully. "Then do not let me die such a lingering death," Florestan pleads.

At the sound of her husband's voice, Fidelio had fallen, fainting, at the side of the grave. Now, concealing her face from him, she hastens forward with a pitcher of wine. Florestan drinks thirstily. "May Heaven bless you," he stammers. "I cannot thank you enough."

"One step and you are dead."

There is a pause. The jailor goes to the stairs and whistles shrilly.

"Is that the signal of my death?" half screams the prisoner, staggering up in his chains. "O, my Leonore, shall I never see you again?"

Fidelio implores him to be calm. Then, as Pizarro descends the stairs and confronts the prisoner, she slips away into the shadows.

"Pizarro stands before you as avenger," the governor cries triumphantly.

Florestan is fearless. "A murderer stands before me," he replies.

The governor raises his dagger. Quickly Fidelio slips in front of him. "Back!" she·cries. "First kill his wife."

"His wife!" Furious at being thwarted by a woman, Pizarro lunges again. But Fidelio whips a pistol out of her pocket. "One step and you are dead," she threatens.

At that instant a trumpet call rings out from the fortress above:

The Minister of Justice has arrived! Soldiers with torches come down to light the governor's way up the stairs and Rocco follows. Florestan and his wife are left alone.

"O, my Leonore," he cries, his voice choked with emotion. "What have you suffered for me?"

"Nothing, nothing, my Florestan," she whispers. They rush into each other's arms, and, weeping with joy, thank God for their happiness:

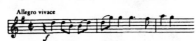

Then, as they turn to leave, the majestic opening chords of the *Leonore Overture No. 3* sweep down the scale. The curtain falls.

This overture is the most famous music from the opera Fidelio *and is often performed in concert. It is like a musical summary of the whole plot. After a slow introduction comes the exciting principal theme:*

This first appears pianissimo, *and works up to a tremendous climax, when the trumpet call, heard in the dungeon scene, peals out again.*

Scene Two. Accompanied by Pizarro, Don Fernando appears on a bastion before the fortress. He is hailed by wild cheers from the towns-people; and the prisoners, who have been brought out of their cells, fall on their knees before him. "I have come to free you from tyranny," the Minister of Justice tells them. "Kneel no longer." As the crowd presses joyously about the newly liberated captives, Rocco pushes his way to the Minister, followed by Florestan and Leonore.

"Florestan!" exclaims Don Fernando in astonishment. "The champion of freedom, in chains! And Leonore!"

"She came to my service disguised as a man," Rocco explains.

Pizarro tries to interrupt, but the Minister silences him. Quickly Rocco describes the scene in the dungeon. "Only your coming saved us," he adds.

The crowd shouts for vengeance, and Pizarro is marched away.

"Now release Florestan," cries Don Fernando. "But wait." He turns to Leonore. "You alone, noblest of women, shall free him of his fetters."

Leonore takes the keys from Rocco. "O, God! What supreme joy!" she whispers, slipping the chains from Florestan's wrists.

He takes her in his arms. "Your loyalty and love have saved me, beloved wife," he cries, and joyously the people raise their voices in a hymn of praise.

The Marriage of Figaro

BY WOLFGANG AMADEUS MOZART

Libretto by Lorenzo da Ponte,
after the French play of Beaumarchais

.

PRINCIPAL CHARACTERS *(in order of appearance):*

Figaro (bass), the clever barber who appeared in Rossini's "Barber of Seville." He is now the servant of Count Almaviva.

Susanna (soprano), the charming but wily young maid-in-waiting to the Countess, betrothed to Figaro.

Bartolo (bass), a spiteful old doctor, the uncle and former guardian of Rosina, who is now Countess Almaviva.

Marcelline (mezzo-soprano), the aged housekeeper of Bartolo, who would like to be rid of her.

Cherubino (soprano), a fickle young page in the Count's service. He is in love with the Countess.

Count Almaviva (baritone), the gallant wooer of Rosina in "The Barber of Seville," now her jealous but not very faithful husband.

Basilio (tenor), the scheming music teacher who once helped Dr. Bartolo in his attempts to wed Rosina. He is employed by the Count to give lessons to Susanna and carry love messages.

The Countess (soprano), no longer the spritely Rosina who played tricks on Uncle Bartolo, but a dignified married lady, who wonders sadly how she can keep her husband from flirting with other women.

PLACE: Count Almaviva's castle, near Seville.   TIME: The eighteenth century.

ACT ONE. The orchestra romps through a gay and sparkling overture that is often heard in concert. Then the curtain rises on a chamber in the castle. Figaro is measuring the room, Susanna is trying on a new bonnet. She asks what he is doing.

"I want to see if the bed will fit into this corner," he answers. "You know, the Count is giving us this handsome chamber. It will be very convenient, too. Should her ladyship want you at night, ding, dong! you can be at her side in a moment. And should his lordship need me, why, ding, dong! in three jumps I am there."

"That is all too true," Susanna remarks. "But beware lest some fine day our master send you on a long errand. Then, ding, dong, perhaps *I* might have a visit from *him*."

"Susanna!" cries Figaro reproachfully.

Laughing at his blindness, she tells him that the Count has been flirting with her for quite a while. The Countess' bell rings, and the girl runs out.

"So!" exclaims Figaro. "That's the way the wind blows. Take care, my lord, the barber can match every plot of yours with a better one."

As Figaro hurries off to make plans for his marriage to Susanna, old Doctor Bartolo enters, accompanied by Marcelline.

"This is not the first wedding I've broken up at the last minute," she tells him. The doctor rubs his hands gleefully.

"How I shall enjoy seeing that knave, Figaro, forced to marry this old witch," he reflects maliciously. "Revenge! That's the thing! . . .

This idiot of a barber imagines I have forgotten that he helped rob me of Rosina, but we shall see who will win—Bartolo or Figaro." He leaves the room.

As Marcelline follows him, she meets Susanna in the doorway. The girl has overheard the old woman, and, curtsying with exaggerated politeness, she makes way for her rival to go through first. "I know my duty to the aged," she says mockingly. The housekeeper goes off in a rage, and Susanna throws a cloak she has been carrying over the back of a large armchair.

Cherubino bursts in. "Susanna, you must help me," he cries. "The Count caught me alone with your cousin, Barbarina, and dismissed me from his service. Unless the Countess intercedes for me I am lost." He notices that Susanna is smoothing out a ribbon from the Countess' headdress, and suddenly snatches it from her. "Dear ribbon, lovely ribbon," he murmurs.

Susanna demands that he return it, but instead the boy gives her a song he has written. "Read it to the Countess," he cries impulsively. "Read it to every girl in the castle. O, Susanna, if you only knew how wildly my heart beats whenever I see a maiden. . . ."

They hear someone coming, and quickly Cherubino slips behind the armchair. Count Almaviva enters.

"Why all this sudden confusion?" he asks the excited girl, sitting down in the chair behind which Cherubino is hiding. Susanna pretends she is afraid somebody will find them together, and begs him to leave. But he refuses. "Meet me in the garden this evening," he urges.

Susanna is about to reply when a high quavering voice is heard outside. The Count dashes behind the armchair just as Cherubino glides around and into it. Susanna covers the boy up with the Countess' cloak and a minute later Don Basilio walks in. "Have you seen the Count?" he asks.

"What have I to do with his lordship?" Susanna replies, trying to hustle him off. The music teacher wags his head maliciously. "He is very fond of you, my dear," he insists, "and anyway I should think you would rather be friends with a gentleman like the Count than with that scalawag, Cherubino."

"O, you horrid slanderer," exclaims the girl.

"Maybe you will tell me about the song, too," Basilio goes on. "Was it for you or the Countess? Anyone can see that Cherubino is in love with her ladyship, and if my lord finds out what people are saying. . . ."

"Well, sir, what *are* people saying?" demands the Count, rising unexpectedly. Both Susanna and Basilio try to defend Cherubino. "Really the poor young fellow has done nothing."

"The poor young fellow!" echoes the Count ironically. "Why, yesterday I caught him with your cousin. The girl didn't want to open the door, and that made me suspicious. So quickly raising the tablecloth. . . ." He lifts up the Countess' robe to show them how he did it. There sits Cherubino.

"What!" shouts the Count. He turns accusingly to Susanna.

The girl explains that Cherubino had come to beg her to obtain the Countess' intervention in his behalf, and, when the Count arrived, hid in terror, first behind the chair. then in it.

At that moment Figaro enters joyously, followed by a crowd of peasants, who sing a song of praise to his lordship. After the singers have left, Cherubino falls on his knees and implores his master's pardon.

"Very well," says the Count. "I make you an ensign in my own regiment. See that you join your men in Seville at once, sir." Almaviva and Basilio depart, leaving the page sunk in gloom.

"Cheer up, my lad," cries Figaro, trying to hearten him. "What a life is open to you now! Instead of hanging idly around the ladies, you will be riding to glory with your fellow heroes."

Allegro

ACT TWO. The Countess paces sadly up and down a magnificent chamber in her apartment, wondering how she can again capture the heart of her husband. "O, god of love, restore him to me," she murmurs.

Susanna enters, and the Countess begs her to finish the story the girl has been telling about Almaviva's attempts to flirt with her. "But he still loves you dearly, I am sure," Susanna insists, "or he would not be so jealous."

Figaro comes in, singing gaily. He tells them that he has sent the Count a letter in which he informs his lordship that the Countess has arranged to meet a certain gentleman at the ball that evening. "In the meantime," he goes on, "I'll tell him that you, Susanna, will meet him in the garden after dark. Then, we'll get Cherubino to delay his departure, put on petticoats, and go in your stead." He runs off to fetch the page, and a few minutes later Cherubino appears.

"Approach, most gallant commander," cries Susanna. The lad sighs.

"Don't remind me that I must leave my kind protectress," he begs, looking ardently at the Countess.

"O, you flatterer!" Susanna mocks. "Here, sir minstrel, sing your ballad to the lady." She hands him the song he had given her, and accompanies him on a guitar.

"What is this feeling that makes me both sad and glad?" sings the page. "Is it love? . . ."

When he has finished, Susanna bolts the door and the two women set about disguising him. "What is this paper?" the Countess asks.

"My commission," he answers, showing it to her.

"It seems they were in such a hurry to get you off that they forgot to seal it," the lady remarks dryly.

Susanna adjusts a cap on Cherubino's head, then goes off with the mantle he has been wearing. As they wait for her to return, there is a knock. "Why are you locked in?" cries the Count, outside. "Open!"

Terrified, Cherubino hides in a cabinet while the Countess goes to let in her husband. Almaviva looks around suspiciously. "I pray you, read that letter, Madame," he says, handing her a paper. It is the note Figaro sent to him. But before the Countess can answer, a chair is upset in the cabinet. "Who is in there?" cries the Count.

"It must be Susanna," his wife answers, in confusion. He tries the door, but it is locked. "Come out, Susanna," he shouts, "or at least answer."

"No, don't answer," cries the Countess. Almaviva is furious.

"We shall soon see whom you have hidden in there," he rages, and, calling to Susanna to await their return, drags the Countess away with him.

The maid has been listening from a place of concealment at the back of the room. Now she calls to Cherubino to come out of the cabinet. To their dismay, they find that the Count has locked them into the room; there is no way for the page to escape except by the window. Leaping out on a garden bed, he leaves Susanna to take his place in the cabinet.

Hardly has she locked herself in, when the Count returns carrying a crowbar. "Well, Madame," he says to the Countess. "Will you unlock the door or shall I break it down?" Tearfully, his wife begs him to be merciful. It is not Susanna who is inside, but a mere child—Cherubino.

In a fury the Count rushes to the cabinet and commands the page to come out. The Countess implores him to spare the boy's life. But he will not listen. "No words can clear you this time," he storms. "Cherubino must die." Finally the door swings open. Out walks Susanna.

Struck dumb with astonishment, the Count and Countess stare at her. "Perhaps the poor page is inside," suggests Susanna ironically, and as Almaviva rushes in to look, she whispers to the Countess that the boy has escaped.

The Count returns, looking very humble. "I have made a mistake, my love," he admits. "Will you forgive me?"

The Countess is not sure she can forget his rudeness, but finally she forgives him, explaining that the tale about Cherubino had been invented to test him, and that Figaro wrote the letter.

The barber enters to announce that all is ready for the wedding.

Cherubino slips behind the chair as the Count enters.

"Wait a minute, my fine fellow," says the Count. "Do you know this letter?"

"Not I, sir," the knave replies. Susanna and the Countess urge him to admit writing it, but in vain. All are about to depart for the festivities when Antonio, the gardener, comes in carrying a broken flower pot.

"Look what has happened to my flowers," he complains to the Count. "A man leaped out of that window there, and crushed all my blossoms."

"I am the man, my lord," declares Figaro hastily. "I was hiding in this room waiting to see Susanna alone when I heard your voice, and fearing your anger jumped out of the window."

"Are these *your* papers?" asks Antonio suspiciously.

The Count snatches them from the gardener. "What is this document?" he asks the barber. Poor Figaro is in a tight place. But peeping over the Count's shoulder, the Countess sees that he holds Cherubino's commission. She whispers to Susanna, and Susanna whispers to Figaro.

"It is Cherubino's commission," the barber declares triumphantly. "He left it with me because. . . ."

"Because what?" demands the Count. The Countess and Susanna signal frantically.

"Because it lacked the seal," finishes Figaro.

The Count is furious at being outwitted again, but just then in come Marcelline, Bartolo, and Basilio.

"Noble Count," cries the old woman, "I demand justice against that scoundrel." She points at Figaro. "He has broken the marriage contract he made with me."

The barber and his friends are horrified. This time it seems as though Figaro were caught.

ACT THREE. The Count is in his study, pondering on the turn of events. "If Susanna has told the Countess about my flirtation with her, Figaro shall marry the old woman," he determines.

Susanna comes in. She pauses to chat with him, and hints that he could help her if he chose by giving the dowry he had promised her to Marcelline to release the barber from his contract.

"When did I promise you a dowry?" asks the Count hastily. "But of course if I did, it was only on condition that you do as I tell you."

"That is my duty," replies the girl, curtsying.

"Then meet me tonight in the garden," he cries eagerly. "O, Susanna, will you come?" She promises to be there, and, as footsteps are heard approaching, the Count slips away. Figaro enters.

"The cause is victorious," Susanna tells him joyfully, and runs off, followed by her bewildered bridegroom. But the Count has heard the girl's words from the back of the room.

"So you plan to deceive me again," he exclaims angrily. "Well, you shall pay dearly, my treacherous beauty. Unless Figaro finds his own ransom money he shall marry Marcelline." Still, the thought that a barber is preferred to him hurts the Count's pride. "Shall my name and rank be rejected?" he cries bitterly. "But my day of vengeance is coming."

Figaro returns with Marcelline, Bartolo, and a notary.

"The dispute is settled," declares the latter. "He must pay or wed her."

"But I am well born, sir," protests Figaro, rolling up his right sleeve. "See, I have the mark of nobility printed on my arm."

Marcelline looks at the mark in greatest excitement. "It is he," she cries to Bartolo. "Our Rafaello."

"Meet your mother, my boy," shouts the doctor, pointing to Marcelline.

"And your father," the old woman replies, pointing to Bartolo.

"By this sign on your arm, we have found not only our son but each other as well," they exult, embracing one another and Figaro.

Susanna comes in. "Here is the ransom money," she says to the Count, handing him a bag. Then she catches sight of Marcelline hugging Figaro. "O you villian," she cries. "So you are deserting me for her."

Marcelline explains that she is Figaro's mother. Furious at the downfall of his plans, the Count leaves, while the others hurry off, rejoicing at the happy ending of their troubles.

Hardly have they left when the Countess comes in another door. "What has happened, I wonder?" she muses. "How did my husband accept Susanna's suggestion?"

She hears voices, and slips out of sight as the Count enters, followed by Antonio. The latter carries Cherubino's regimental hat.

"The boy is still in the castle, my lord," insists the gardener. "And this hat is the proof of it. Come this way, and you will surely catch him." They hasten out.

Susanna and the Countess come in. "What did he say?" the lady asks.

"O, he muttered something about revenge," the girl replies.

"Good," cries the Countess. "Now write this letter, my child." Susanna sits down at the writing-table. "Hither, gentle zephyr," the Countess dictates. "Come to the spot where the rose and myrtle grow...."

That is all. He will understand the message."

Susanna fastens the note with a pin. "Write on the outside that he should return the pin," the Countess tells her. The girl writes.

Susanna hides the note quickly as a band of peasant girls flocks into the room. Among them is Cherubino, disguised as a maiden. While the peasants are singing a song to the Countess, the Count and Antonio return. Immediately the gardener hauls Cherubino forward, pulls off his bonnet, and sets the regimental cap on his head. "There is your soldier," he declares gruffly.

Poor Cherubino stands trembling with fright, and the Count is about to punish him, when Figaro bursts in. "My lord, you are delaying the festivities." A march is heard in the distance. The peasants rush out, followed by Cherubino, Susanna, and Figaro.

As the Count and his lady take their places on the thrones at one side of the room, the curtains at the back are lifted. Beyond is a splendid hall and a great marble staircase.

The bridal procession comes down the stairs, and Susanna kneels before the Count, who places the bridal veil upon her head. As he does so, she slyly slips him the Countess' note. Then Figaro draws her aside to watch the peasants dance.

Meanwhile the Count reads his note. "I understand, my dear," he whispers, folding it up hastily. But Figaro has seen him. "Still another love note, no doubt," he says to Susanna with a laugh.

ACT FOUR. Susanna's little cousin, Barbarina, comes into a secluded spot in the castle gardens, searching for something on the ground. "O, unlucky little needle," she wails. "Where have you hidden yourself?"

"What are you looking for?" asks Figaro, coming up with Marcelline.

"Why, for the pin his lordship told me to take to Susanna," the child replies. She runs off.

Poor Figaro has turned pale. "That pin was the same one I saw with the Count's letter," he tells his mother sorrowfully. She departs, telling him not to worry about it too much, and the barber is left alone in the dark, silent garden.

"Who would have thought that I should ever play the part of the jealous, cheated husband?" he reflects despairingly. "And who would have believed that you would betray me, Susanna . . . ?

O, it is folly to put one's faith in a woman. They are all deceivers, every one."

He conceals himself quickly as Susanna, disguised as the Countess, creeps softly along the garden path. After her comes the Countess, disguised as Susanna. Marcelline is with them, and she, too, hides.

Susanna and the Countess confer for a moment in whispers, then the latter slips into a pavilion that stands at the right. Susanna seats herself under the linden trees to enjoy the breeze. "Come to me, my dearest," she sighs. "At last you shall be all mine. . . ."

Cherubino enters, singing. At once the Countess comes forward. "Why, Susanna!" exclaims the boy joyfully, as he recognizes the maid's dress. He tries to kiss her, but the Count, who has stolen unnoticed along the path, rushes forward.

"Take that, you little snake," he shouts angrily, trying to box the page on the ear, but Figaro, who has also rushed forward, receives it instead. The barber slinks back to the bushes and Cherubino takes the opportunity of scampering away. The Countess, disguised as Susanna, and her husband are left alone.

"How soft and lovely your hands are, Susanna," whispers the Count. He takes a diamond ring from his finger and slips it on hers. Torches gleam in the distance, and he draws her toward a near-by grove.

Figaro, Marcelline, and the real Susanna have all been watching from separate hiding places, but only the barber does not know that the girl with whom the Count is flirting is the Countess and not his own Susanna. When he sees the two start toward the grove he springs up furiously. "Why," he mutters, "she is actually going with him."

The Count hears the barber moving about in the dark and asks who is there. At once the Countess runs into the pavilion at the right. The Count follows her, but as Figaro prepares to give chase, Susanna, dressed in the Countess' clothes, stops him.

"Ha!" cries the angry man. "The Countess, no less. Madame, Susanna is with his lordship. Come see for yourself."

But now Susanna is angry that her bridegroom does not trust her, and, forgetting to disguise her voice, she declares she will not go.

"Susanna!" exclaims Figaro, in glad surprise. At that moment the Count returns, looking for the supposed maid-in-waiting, who has escaped him. Quickly the barber kneels before Susanna. "Ah, Countess," he cries ardently. "I love you with all my heart."

"I am yours, beloved," the girl replies, imitating the Countess' voice.

"O, the traitors," shouts the Count, enraged, and as they start off he catches the barber by the cloak. Susanna escapes into the right-hand pavilion. Basilio, Antonio, and the notary hurry up in response to the Count's shouts. Telling them to hold Figaro, Almaviva rushes madly into the dark pavilion after his supposed wife. But when he comes out he finds to his fury that he is clutching Cherubino. Again he rushes in, and this time he drags out Susanna, who hides her face in her hands.

Figaro and Susanna plead for mercy, but the Count rages and storms. No, he will never forgive them.

Then the Countess, still dressed as her maid, comes forward quietly. She kneels at the Count's feet and, with an air of playful malice, asks: "Will not Susanna's prayers win your mercy?"

Astonished and confused, the Count hardly knows what to say. "Forgive me, my angel," he cries at last. "I have behaved unworthily." The Countess forgives him gladly, and happily all return to the castle.

Hansel and Gretel*

BY ENGELBERT HUMPERDINCK

*Libretto by Adelheid Wette,
based on a Grimms' fairy tale*

PRINCIPAL CHARACTERS *(in order of appearance):*

Gretel (soprano), a little girl.

Hansel (mezzo-soprano), her light-hearted but lazy brother.

Gertrude (mezzo-soprano), their mother.

Peter (baritone), her husband, a jovial, good-natured broom-maker.

The Sandman (soprano), a kindly wood-fairy.

The Dewman (soprano), another wood-fairy.

The Wicked Witch (mezzo-soprano).

PLACE: A forest in Germany.   TIME: The days of witches and fairies.

THE PRELUDE is like a musical sketch of the story. It begins with the melody of the *Children's Prayer*, which appears in every scene of the opera:

Then comes a spritely little theme:

*Musical quotations by permission of Associated Music Publishers, Inc., owners of the copyright.

This is the *Witch's Magic Charm* turned upside down, and it is used this way whenever anybody is released from enchantment. After that appears a slow, lovely melody, describing *Dawn* in the wood:

Last of all comes a theme of rejoicing:

ACT ONE. *Scene One.* The curtain rises on a room in Peter's house on the edge of the forest. Gretel is busy knitting a stocking, Hansel is making a broom.

"Susy, little Susy, pray what is the news?" sings Gretel.

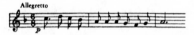

"The geese are going barefoot because they've no shoes."

"What I want to know is who will give me some sugar and bread?" sings her brother, throwing away his broom. "Not a thing to eat for weeks but dry crusts!"

"Hush, Hansel," replies Gretel. "Remember what father has told us:
       'When in direst need we stand,
       God will offer us His hand.'"

"That's all very well," the boy retorts, "but we can't eat verses."

Gretel seizes the broom and chases him around the room. "You bad boy, always grumbling. . . . Hansel, would you like to know a secret?" She shows him a jug full of milk. "Our neighbor gave it to us, and Mother will surely make a fine pudding when she comes home."

"Goody!" shouts Hansel, jumping up and down gleefully. "Come on, Gretel, let's dance. No more work today." She joins him gaily.

"Brother dear, come dance with me, here are both my hands, you see. Right foot first, left foot then, whirl about and back again."

The children stop in their tracks.

At the height of the excitement in comes their mother.

"Why, what's all this?" She catches sight of the unfinished broom and neglected stocking. "You naughty children!" she exclaims angrily. "Here Father and I work from morning till night and you do nothing but dance and sing." In her vexation she gives the milk jug a shove with her elbow. It crashes to the floor in a hundred pieces.

"O, deary me!" the poor woman cries, bursting into tears. "There goes our supper." She looks at the milk streaming down her skirt. Hansel titters.

"What! Laughing at me, you little good-for-nothing!" she screams furiously. "Off with the two of you into the woods, and see that you bring home a basketful of berries." As the children scamper out, Gertrude sits down wearily.

"Now what shall I do?" she wails. "There's not a crumb in the house for my poor starving children. Dear Lord, send me help. . . ." Leaning on the table, she falls asleep.

"Tra-la-la-la, little mother, I am here," bellows a cheerful voice outside.

Peter staggers in, carrying a large basket. He wakes his wife with a resounding kiss. "What are we going to eat today, my dear?"

Gertrude pushes him away angrily. "When the larder is empty there's not much choice."

Laughing, Peter shows her the contents of his basket—ham, butter, sausage, potatoes, even a dozen eggs, and, as she bustles about preparing supper, he tells her of his good luck in town. Suddenly he stops short.

"Where are the children?"

Gertrude explains about the milk jug, and Peter laughs heartily. But when she tells him that she sent the children to the forest to gather berries, he snatches a broom from the wall in alarm. An ominous melody sounds in the orchestra:

It is the theme of the *Witch's Broomstick*.

"Don't you know that a wicked old witch lives in the wood?" gasps Peter.

"At midnight she rides on her broomstick, but by day she catches children and bakes them into gingerbread in her red-hot oven " Gertrude wrings her hands in despair.

"We must find them," Peter cries, and, as they rush out, the curtain falls quickly.

At once the broomstick theme sounds again, loud and furious, as though the witches were gathering for their ghostly flight over hill and dale, and a minute later the wild rhythms of the *Witches' Ride* sweep through the orchestra:

Finally the music calms down. A murmuring suggests rustling leaves, and the curtain rises on a mossy dell in the midst of the forest.

Scene Two. Gretel is busy weaving a garland of wild roses.

"A little man stands in the woods all alone," she sings. "He wears a purple cloak and a little black cap."

"My basket is full," interrupts Hansel, running in. Gretel tries to put her wreath on his head, but he crowns her with it instead.

At that moment a bird calls softly in the distance. "Cuckoo! Cuckoo!"

"Cuckoo, where are you?" shout the children gaily.

"He is a thief and eats other birds' eggs," Hansel declares.

"Like that?" asks Gretel, sticking a berry in his mouth. They start eating, both grabbing at the basket until finally Hansel yanks it away and pours the remainder of the berries into his mouth.

"O, Hansel!" cries Gretel, horrified. "Whatever will Mother say?"

"Well, it's too dark to find any more now," the boy replies uneasily, and begins looking around for the path home.

Suddenly the cuckoo calls from the bushes right behind them.

"What was that noise?" cries Hansel, startled. He turns to his sister in despair. "Gretel, I can't find the way."

The shadows have deepened and will-o'-the-wisps flicker through the shrubbery. Fearfully Gretel peers about.

"What is that glimmering over there?" she screams, pointing at a weird shape in the gloom.

"Why, only a s-s-silver birch. . . ." Hansel stammers. "Wait, Gretel, I'll give a good loud call. . . . Who's there?" he shouts.

"YOOooooouuuu there!" echoes mysteriously through the dark woods. Terrified, the children cling to each other. A thick mist has risen and covers the trees at the back, but now it lifts a bit, and a little gray man slips through.

"I am the Sandman," he whispers, sprinkling sand from the sack on his back into the children's eyes. "Go to sleep, my dearies. The angels in Heaven will watch over you."

As the little man vanishes, the children kneel sleepily and repeat their Evening Prayer:

> *"When at night I go to sleep,*
> *Fourteen angels watch do keep."*

They sink down on the mossy ground with their arms about each other.

Suddenly a bright light breaks through the mist, and a magic stairway seems to rise up through the trees to Heaven. Down it come fourteen angels. Two by two, they step to earth and group themselves about the sleeping children.

ACT TWO. The prelude begins with an odd little questioning theme:

"Who's nibbling at my house-kin?" it seems to ask over and over again. Then the mood changes. The *Dawn* melody that appeared in the Prelude to Act One returns, and the curtain rises again on the dell in the forest.

Morning is breaking. The Dewman shakes drops from a bluebell over the sleeping children. As they begin to stir, he hurries off into the mist at the back. Gretel wakes first. The birds are twittering in the trees, and she tries to chirp like a lark.

"Ti-re-li-re-li," she warbles merrily.

Hansel bounces up. "Ki-ke-ri-ki," he crows, pretending to be a rooster.

The children start to talk about the dream they had in the night. Fourteen angels came down a stairway right back there, they agree excitedly, and turn to look.

There stands a most wonderful little house. The mist has cleared away, and the rising sun shines brightly on its plumcake walls and quaint gables bulging with raisins. Hansel and Gretel are speechless with astonishment.

"The angels must have guided us here," they burst out at last, and skipping past the gingerbread fence they break off pieces of the plumcake wall.

"Nibble, nibble, mouse-kin, who's nibbling at my house-kin?" sings a funny little voice. Startled, the children look about them.

"It must have been the wind," they decide, breaking off some more cake. The upper part of the door opens, and the witch pokes out her head. But the children are far too busy eating to notice her and, slipping up behind them, she throws a rope around Hansel's neck.

"Let me go," shouts the boy, struggling violently.

The witch smacks her lips. "Mmmm, what tender morsels you both will be after I've fattened you up," she gloats. "Come with me, my darlings. I'll give you sweetmeats and dainties to your hearts' delight."

Hansel has finally managed to free himself; seizing Gretel's hand, he starts to run. At once the old hag snatches a juniper wand from her belt and waves it. "Hocus pocus, witch's charm!" she cries.

The children stop in their tracks. Triumphantly, the witch thrusts Hansel into a cage at one side and orders Gretel to set the table. While the girl is in the house, the witch looks in the oven.

"I'll eat Gretel first," she decides. "How delicious she will taste!"

Then, in wild delight, she seizes a broomstick and begins to ride on it. A mysterious darkness descends over the wood. Suddenly, with a scream, the witch sails over the housetop.

No sooner has she descended than daylight returns. She hobbles over to the cage.

"Show me your thumb," says she. Hansel pokes out a small bone.

"My goodness!" exclaims his captor. "How skinny you are. Gretel, fetch some almonds and raisins."

While the witch is feeding him, Gretel, who has discovered a juniper bush and made herself a wand, waves the stick in the direction of her brother. "Hocus pocus, elder-bush!" she mutters.

"What's that, my little miss?" croaks the witch, turning around suddenly. She goes over to the oven, and Hansel, who has been freed by Gretel's magic spell, hides behind his sister.

"Come here and look inside to see if the gingerbread is ready," the witch commands Gretel. But the girl pretends not to understand.

"Show me what you mean," she begs.

Muttering angrily, the old hag peers inside the glowing oven. Quick as a flash Hansel and Gretel push from behind. In goes the witch. Slamming the door, the children dance about gaily.

"The witch is dead," they shout. Suddenly there is a terrific explosion, and the oven falls to pieces.

When the dust settles, Hansel and Gretel notice to their astonishment that the gingerbread fence has vanished. In its place is a row of children, standing stiff and stark with closed eyes.

"Hocus pocus, elder-bush!" cries Hansel, waving the juniper wand, and immediately the children flock about their rescuers, dancing and singing.

At that moment a lusty voice is heard singing in the woods. Peter bursts upon the scene, followed by his wife, and Hansel and Gretel throw themselves into their arms. Meanwhile two of the boys have dragged an enormous gingerbread figure out of the ruins of the oven. It is the wicked witch. Everyone gives a shout of joy at the sight, then one and all join in a hymn of thanksgiving:

> *"When in direst need we stand,*
> *God will offer us His hand."*

Lohengrin

BY RICHARD WAGNER

Libretto by the composer

PRINCIPAL CHARACTERS (in order of appearance):

King Henry the Fowler (bass), ruler of Germany, who has come to Brabant to seek military support for his war against the Huns.

Friedrich Telramund (baritone), a proud and ambitious knight of Brabant, in whose care the late Duke left the guidance of the realm during the youth of his children, Elsa and Godfrey.

Ortrud (mezzo-soprano), wife of Telramund. Mistress of the black art of magic, she has gained a fateful influence over her husband.

Elsa (soprano), the young Duchess of Brabant.

Lohengrin (tenor), mysterious knight of the swan.

PLACE: The Duchy of Brabant, near the great medieval city of Antwerp, Belgium.

TIME: The early tenth-century, when knights sought and served the Holy Grail.

PRELUDE. From the orchestra comes an ethereal melody:

"My deliverer," cries Elsa, "I shall always trust and obey you."

It is the *Holy Grail*, borne down to earth. and this theme fills all the prelude. Instrument after instrument adds its voice, the music expands until the whole air seems filled with radiance. There is a dazzling burst of sound. Then the Grail is drawn up again to Heaven.

THE FIRST ACT opens on the banks of the winding River Scheldt. Everywhere are warriors, and the air is gay with pennants. King Henry is seated under a tree, surrounded by his followers. He has come to call the men of Brabant to his banner. but he finds the Duchy in confusion, shaken by rumors of a mysterious crime. "What is the cause of all this unrest?" he asks Friedrich Telramund.

"The heir of Brabant has disappeared." answers Telramund. And he tells how Elsa wandered into the woods one day with the young prince. Returning alone, she claimed to have lost the boy in the forest, but her guilty distress betrayed her crime.

"In horror," cries Telramund, "I drew back from my proposed marriage with her."

Then he turns to a dark, imperious woman, dressed in rich apparel, who sits at one side, and presents her to the King. It is Ortrud, haughty daughter of the Prince of Friesland, whom he has married instead.

"Elsa is guilty of her brother's murder," Telramund continues. "And as next of kin I claim the Duchy of Brabant."

Horrified, the King calls upon Elsa to defend herself, and she comes up from the river bank, surrounded by her maidens.

Everyone is struck by her beauty and simplicity. It seems inconceivable that she could be guilty of such a crime. But when the King questions her, Elsa tells him of a knight in shining armor who appeared to her in a dream.

"Her accomplice!" cries Telramund, and he declares himself ready to defend his accusation with his life. Elsa puts her trust in the champion of her dreams.

Then the trumpeters peal their summons to the four winds, and the King's herald calls upon Elsa's knight to appear. There follows tense silence, but no champion appears. It is the judgment of Heaven.

Elsa flings herself on her knees. "You who sent him to me in my dreams," she prays, "bid him help me now in my desperate need."

As she finishes shouts are heard from the river bank. "Look, look, a swan! A swan drawing a boat!" Others rush to the shore. "A knight stands in the boat," they cry.

Elsa listens as though in a dream. She dares not look, but Ortrud and Telramund push through the excited crowd. They return amazed and terrified.

There, at the back, is a skiff drawn by a beautiful white swan. And in it is a knight clad in shining silver armor.

He steps ashore. "Farewell, my faithful swan," he cries.

Then, turning to the King, he declares himself ready to prove Elsa's innocence. He makes only one condition: she must never attempt to discover *his name or from what country he has come.*

If she will promise that before them all, he will be her champion.

"My deliverer," cries Elsa, kneeling before him, "as you defend me today, so shall I always trust and obey you."

The place of combat is then measured off, the King calls upon God to defend the right, and the fight begins. Both men strive furiously, but, with a sudden blow, the swan knight crushes his foe to the ground. Ortrud has watched with growing despair. "Who is this man?" she ponders. "With what art does he destroy my power?"

Now the knight turns to Elsa. Radiant with joy, she throws herself into his arms, and together they greet the King. Women press about waving garlands, the men of Brabant lift Elsa and her knight on their shields, and in triumph all set out for the castle.

THE SECOND ACT opens with dark, sinister music suggestive of treachery. A new theme, *Doubt*, appears:

Then the *Motive of the Forbidden Question*, heard in the first act, sounds ominously in the wind instruments.

Night hangs over the citadel of Antwerp. On the steps of the cathedral, facing the royal dwelling, sit two sombre figures. half lost in dense shadow. They are Ortrud and the defeated Telramund. "Let us flee," he cries, rising in despair. But Ortrud cannot flee. She stares at the windows of the castle, from which ring out sounds of merriment and rejoicing. Then she discloses her sinister plans to her husband. "This strange knight, who has come so mysteriously," she whispers, "is protected by magic. Let Elsa, whom he has forbidden to ask his name, but question him, and all his strength will be shattered."

Just then a light from above pierces the gloom. Elsa comes out onto her balcony. "O you wandering breezes, who have so often listened to my grief," she cries, "see my joy today."

Ortrud interrupts her. "Elsa," she calls mournfully from the court below, "how have I harmed you that I should be driven away now in shame and want?"

Elsa is horrified at the reproach. She hastens to let Ortrud in.

Telramund has slipped away, and in that moment Ortrud is alone. She springs from the cathedral steps, a figure of fury and vengeance. "Wotan, Freia," she screams, hurling her supplications into the black night, "lend me your pagan might!"

The next minute the door opens, and she sinks at Elsa's feet. "O, do not kneel before me," cries Elsa, overcome by Ortrud's forlorn appearance. She comforts Ortrud with promises of the swan knight's forgiveness.

Ortrud is humble. "How can I thank you?" she protests. "If only I could save you from misfortune. May he who came to you so miraculously never leave you by the same magic art."

Elsa is startled. But no, her faith is unshakeable, she will not doubt. They enter the castle together.

Day dawns, and gradually the nobles of Brabant assemble. The King's herald appears. "By the King's decree Friedrich Telramund is banished from the land." he declares. "His conqueror desires to be known as the Protector of Brabant, and tomorrow he will lead you to the wars behind the banner of the King."

The shouts of the nobles are interrupted by the bridal procession. First come pages, then the ladies of the court. All eyes are turned toward the royal dwelling. At last Elsa appears at the doorway in her white bridal robes, and the chorus swells to a hymn of joy. She descends the steps, followed by Ortrud, now regally clad. They cross the court, they mount the cathedral steps. Suddenly Ortrud hastens forward. "Back, Elsa." she cries. and faces the crowd with flashing eyes. "Shall I bow before the bride of a nameless adventurer, who, in cunning, hides his identity?"

Her bitter words are interrupted by the appearance of King Henry and the swan knight. The bridal procession is reformed, and all proceed toward the cathedral. But at the doorway the pages spring back. Friedrich Telramund, robed in black, stands on the threshold. "Away with him," shouts the crowd. But he silences it with a gesture.

"Who is this knight that came to us upon the water?" he demands. "By magic he has defied the might of God. If he is true. then let him reveal his name."

In tense excitement the crowd turns to the swan knight. But he disregards Friedrich's question; he must give an answer to Elsa alone. And Elsa is torn by doubt.

"My beloved," cries the knight in anguish, "in your hands rests all our happiness. Will you ask me this fatal question?"

But she pulls herself together. "Doubt shall never conquer my love," she replies.

The organ in the cathedral peals out, the trumpeters on the castle walls sound a brilliant fanfare. "Hail, Elsa of Brabant," cry the people exultantly. But, as the bridal couple reach the church portal, Elsa glances back. Ortrud stands in the midst of the throng, her clenched fist raised in triumph, and the orchestra thunders out the *Motive of the Forbidden Question.*

THE THIRD ACT Prelude is dominated by a brilliant, strident theme, describing the wedding feast.

Then the music becomes softer, and voices are heard, chanting a nuptial song:

The First Scene opens on a bridal chamber in the castle. Moonlight streams in the open window.

Presently the wedding party enters. A brief ceremony follows, then the lovers are left alone. They whisper to each other of their love. But the mystery of her knight's name torments Elsa. She fears he will forsake her and return to the land from which he came.

Suddenly she fancies that she sees the swan. There, there, floating on the river, calling him away! Wildly she turns to the knight. "I must know your name and country," she cries desperately, "even though it cost me my life."

At that moment Telramund breaks through the door, sword in hand. The swan knight slays him with a stroke. Then, turning to Telramund's accomplices, who have fallen on their knees before him, he instructs them to carry the slain man to the King's judgment seat. There he will also answer Elsa. Wearily the orchestra echoes the *Motive of the Forbidden Question,* and the curtain falls.

The Final Scene of the opera takes place by the banks of the Scheldt. Horsemen and men-at-arms throng the meadow; the nobles of Brabant are gathering their retainers for departure to the war. Finally the King enters, greeted by the blare of trumpets and cheers of the assembled troops. All now await the Protector of Brabant.

The crowd separates, and the four accomplices of Telramund bear the body of the slain Count before the King. They are closely followed by Elsa. At last, shouts are heard in the rear: "Make way, make way for the hero of Brabant." The swan knight, in full armor, strides forward.

But he cannot lead them to battle. Silencing their protests, he tells them of the treacherous attack of Telramund and of Elsa's betrayal. "All of you heard her promise never to ask my name and rank," he declares sternly. "She has broken that sacred oath, and I must answer."

Awe-struck and fearful, the people wait in silence. From the orchestra steal whispered harmonies of the Holy Grail. Then the swan knight tells them of a distant land. There, on shores untouched by mortal feet, stands the castle of Montsalvat, guarding a mystic cup. It is the Grail, brought down from Heaven by angels, and it gives supernatural strength to the knights who serve it. They are sent out into the world to defend the innocent, but they must remain unknown to those they help. For if once their secret is discovered, the spell is broken and they must depart.

"So now I answer the fatal question," he concludes. "My father, Parsifal, reigns in Montsalvat. I am his knight, and Lohengrin is my name."

Deeply stirred, the crowd bows before him. Elsa sinks fainting into his arms. "My dearest wife," cries Lohengrin, "why did you wring the question from me? Now I must go. . . ."

In vain all implore him to stay. From the river bank come shouts, "The swan! The swan!"

Lohengrin goes to the shore and greets the swan sadly. Then he turns. "O, Elsa," he laments, "had you only been true one brief year, the power of the Grail would have restored your brother to you. But should he return, give him these tokens—this horn and sword to help him in danger, this ring to remind him of me. Now farewell." He embraces her passionately. "The Grail calls, and I must go."

As he strides toward the swan boat, Ortrud pushes her way furiously through the crowd. "Depart, proud hero," she screams in triumph. "But he who draws you. the swan, is the victim of *my* enchantment—it is Godfrey of Brabant that takes you away from Elsa."

The people shrink back from her in horror. Lohengrin sinks to his knees in prayer. Suddenly, a white dove flutters down over the bank. Lohengrin springs up, and, as he unfastens the golden chain from about the swan's neck, the bird sinks beneath the water. In its place Lohengrin lifts to shore a beautiful youth. "Behold, the Duke of Brabant!" he cries, and steps into the skiff, which is led off down the river by the dove.

The nobles of Brabant bend the knee in homage to their young lord.

Elsa embraces her brother. Then she rushes to the shore. Lohengrin has disappeared. "My knight, my husband!" she cries, and sinks lifeless to the ground.

Lucia di Lammermoor

BY GAETANO DONIZETTI

Libretto by Commarano, based on Sir Walter Scott's novel,
"The Bride of Lammermoor"

PRINCIPAL CHARACTERS *(in order of appearance)*:

Lord Henry Ashton (baritone), a hot-tempered and vengeful Scottish nobleman, who for many years has waged a bitter feud against a neighboring clan, the Ravenswoods. Now Lord Henry is threatened by a political catastrophe.

Raymond (bass), the kind-hearted elderly tutor of Henry's sister, Lucia.

Norman (tenor), captain of Lord Ashton's retainers.

Lucia Ashton (soprano), a beautiful young woman, whose hand in marriage her brother wants to give for his political advantage.

Edgar of Ravenswood (tenor), a fearless young Scotsman.

Lord Arthur Bucklaw (tenor), an influential nobleman, in high favor at court, with whom Lord Henry hopes to form an alliance.

PLACE: Scotland.   TIME: About 1700.

ACT ONE. After a brief, gloomy prelude, the curtain rises on a desolate spot in the grounds surrounding the ancient castle of Ravenswood, which Lord Henry has wrested from young Edgar, the only surviving member of the Ravenswood clan. Lord Henry paces restlessly up and down, accompanied by Raymond and Norman.

"My fortunes are definitely waning," the nobleman bursts out at last. "Only Lucia can save me. She must be forced to wed."

"The poor child is still mourning the death of her mother," replies

Raymond. "How can you think of forcing thoughts of love on her at such a time?"

Norman laughs mockingly. "Thoughts of love! Why, she is in love at this very moment." He tells his startled companions how Lucia was saved from a wild bull by the bullet of a stranger, who now meets her secretly every day in the park.

"His name?" interrupts Lord Henry, fearfully.

It is Edgar of Ravenswood. Norman's accusation is supported by the guards, who have seen the young man lurking in the neighborhood, and angrily Lord Henry vows to be avenged on both the perfidy of his sister and the insolent daring of his foe. Raymond begs him not to act in anger, but he pleads in vain.

"The wretches shall pay for their guilty love with their lives," shouts the nobleman,

and storms off, followed by his men. Heavy-hearted, Raymond returns to the castle.

Dusk has fallen, and a ruined well, half hidden in the tangled underbrush, is shrouded in mysterious half-light. Lucia and her companion, Alice, slip silently into the clearing.

"Where are you leading me?" whispers Alice. "If your brother should find you, his wrath will be terrible."

"I know. I know," replies Lucia, glancing about nervously. "But I must warn Edgar of his danger." She sees the ruined well, and starts back in fear. "That fountain! O, Alice, I can never look at it without trembling." She tells her friend that the place is haunted by the ghost of a maiden who was murdered there years ago by her jealous lover and flung into the well. Once, she, Lucia, had seen the phantom on a moonlight night, and it had waved its bloodless hand as though warning her of some terrible fate. . . .

The girl's thoughts turn to Edgar Ravenswood. For her brother's sake she should try to forget him, but she cannot. "He is the master of my heart," she cries passionately. "What happier lot could I ask than to be with him?"

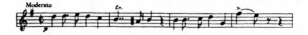

A figure is seen approaching in the shadows, and Alice slips off to keep watch. Edgar hastens in.

"Forgive me for asking you to meet me here at such an hour," he whispers, embracing Lucia. "But I am obliged to leave Scotland at once on a political mission, and had to see you first, my darling. Can we not be married before I leave?"

"My brother would never permit it," she falters.

"Then he is not yet satisfied with all the misfortunes he has brought upon me?" Edgar cries bitterly. "First he slays my father, then steals my estate. Will he have my life as well?" Lucia tries to calm him, assuring him of her love.

Edgar slips a ring on her finger. "With this token I pledge my faith before the altar of Heaven," he declares. "Lucia, you are mine."

"And you are mine, beloved," she answers, giving him a token in return.

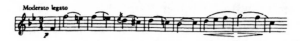

He sweeps her into his arms. "Farewell, my dearest. I must go. But the day will come when I shall return and claim you as my bride."

ACT TWO, *Scene One.* In an apartment of the castle, Lord Henry is talking with his henchman, Norman. "All my kindred have gathered to celebrate Lucia's wedding," he observes uneasily. "Lord Arthur Bucklaw, whom I have been most fortunate in securing for a brother-in-law, will soon be here. But what if my sister should persist in her refusal to marry?"

"Have no fear!" replies the captain. "She will not refuse. We have intercepted all Edgar's letters, and certainly his long silence must have raised some doubts in her heart. When she sees this forged message

telling of his union with another, I am sure she will do as you wish."
They see Lucia approaching, and Norman hastens off.

The girl reproaches her brother for trying to force her into wedlock.
"I can never marry this man," she insists. "My faith is pledged to
Edgar."

Lord Henry hands her the forged letter. "Read that, and see what
a traitor you have for a lover."

Lucia snatches the paper from him. "It cannot be true," she gasps,
turning pale. But the evidence is clear. Suddenly festal music is heard
in the distance. "What is that?" she cries, starting.

"The welcome to your bridegroom," her brother replies triumphantly. "Hasten now, and prepare for your nuptials."

"Ah, never!" she half shrieks.

Lord Henry seizes her savagely by the arm. "Listen, Lucia. The
death of the King has sealed my doom, and only this alliance with Lord
Bucklaw can rescue me from the scaffold. You must save me!" She
cowers before him. "My ghost will haunt you. . . ," he threatens.

Raymond hastens in. "There is no more hope," he tells the despairing girl. "Your lover is false. O, I implore you, by the memory of your
dear mother, to come to the assistance of Lord Henry."

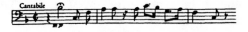

At last Lucia surrenders. Weeping, she goes to prepare for her wedding.

Scene Two. The guests have gathered in the great hall of the castle,
and greet Lord Arthur Bucklaw with joyous acclaim.

Finally the bride appears. Pale and tearful, she is hurried to the altar,
and the marriage contract is signed. But hardly has Lucia laid down

the pen when a thundering is heard at the castle gate. Edgar has returned to claim his bride.

He stops in horror on the threshold. "What do I see? Have you betrayed me?"

Despairing. Lucia turns from him. "Where shall I hide myself?" she moans. "Ah, I am doomed, doomed." Her brother and Lord Arthur draw their swords, ordering Edgar from the castle. But he wheels on them fiercely.

"She is mine. Our vows were plighted before Heaven."

Raymond shows him the marriage contract. "What! Signed by you, Lucia?" cries the young man, and tears her ring from his finger. "Take back your faithless love," he raves, dashing the token at her feet. "Be accursed!"

The crowd roars for vengeance, but Raymond halts them, and, turning on his heel, Edgar strides out of the hall. Lucia sinks fainting to the ground.

ACT THREE, *Scene One.* The great hall of Lammermoor rings with the noise of revelry as the wedding guests celebrate far into the night. "Hail, Scotland." they shout joyously. "Fortune shall shine on you. . . ."

Abruptly, Raymond appears on the threshold, his face white and drawn. He bids them be silent. "You all saw Lucia retire to her room," he says hoarsely. "Ah, listen to what has befallen in this night of woe.

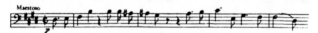

While you were feasting so merrily, a fearful shriek rang out from the bridal chamber. I hastened to the place, and there beheld Lord Arthur stretched lifeless before me. Over him stood his bride. Lucia. a bloodstained sword in her hand. 'Where is my husband?' she muttered, a senseless smile on her pallid face. O pity her, she has gone mad!"

The wedding guests gasp in horror, then turn quickly as a step is heard. Lucia stands in the doorway.

"Take back your faithless love,"
raves Edgar. "Be accursed!"

"I hear his voice," she murmurs. "Edgar, my beloved, I am yours."
Suddenly, the girl stares before her in terror. "The phantom! It rises
from the well to part us. Edgar. . . . Yet we shall meet at the altar.
Hark to the nuptial hymn, my dearest. See, the tapers are lighted and
the priest is ready. . . . O, day of joy!"

Lord Henry bursts into the hall. "Did you do this foul deed?" he
demands of his sister, furiously. Lucia quails before him.

"Yes, truly, I did sign the contract," she mutters. "He cursed me! Ah, I am the victim of a cruel brother. . . . But I love you, Edgar. Do not leave me with this Arthur. Do not leave me. . . ."

Horrified at the consequences of his own deed, Lord Henry turns away. Lucia sinks unconscious in the arms of her attendants.

Scene Two. Brooding over Lucia's marriage, Edgar wanders through the wild, gloomy moorland among the tombs of his ancestors. His anger is gone, and now, desperate, he seeks only death. In the distance, the lights of the castle gleam fitfully.

"Dance on, wanton," Edgar cries bitterly. "Rejoice with your husband. I shall find my joy here in the grave."

Suddenly he notices a procession of mourners coming from Lammermoor. Their sorrowful chant strikes cold fear into his heart, and as they pass he asks anxiously for whom they weep.

"For Lucia," answer the grief-stricken retainers. "She has gone mad, and in her last delirium calls for you, Edgar Ravenswood." Even as they speak, the sound of tolling bells echoes across the moor.

"I must see her once more," cries the young man. Frantically he pushes past the mourners. His way is barred by Raymond, who has approached unnoticed.

"Where are you hastening?" the old tutor asks sadly. "Lucia is dead."

"Dead!" cries Edgar. "My beloved Lucia, dead! Ah, then I will follow you. . . ."

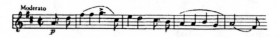

He draws his sword wildly, and, before the horrified retainers can prevent him, plunges the blade into his own heart.

Die Meistersinger

BY RICHARD WAGNER

Libretto by the composer

PRINCIPAL CHARACTERS *(in order of appearance):*

Walther von Stolzing (tenor), a young knight, who has come to Nuremberg to see Veit Pogner on business, and has fallen in love with the burgher's daughter.

Eva (soprano), the charming young daughter of Pogner.

Magdalene (mezzo-soprano), her nurse, in love with the youth David.

David (tenor), the impudent young apprentice of Hans Sachs.

Veit Pogner (bass), a wealthy goldsmith.

Sixtus Beckmesser (baritone), the Town Clerk, a malicious, quarrelsome fellow, who is eager to win the hand of Eva.

Hans Sachs (bass-baritone), kind-hearted and much loved cobbler-poet of Nuremberg. (Sachs was a real poet, who wrote over four thousand poems.)

PLACE: The medieval town of Nuremberg.   TIME: Middle of the sixteenth century.

The Prelude begins with the pompous theme of the *Mastersingers of Nuremberg*—worthy master craftsmen, who have formed a guild devoted to song-making:

After it appears a lyric melody, voicing the impetuous wooing of Walther:

This, in turn, is interrupted by a fanfare, the *Mastersingers' March,* which is an actual tune from the sixteenth century:

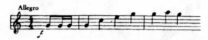

Then the violins whisper a lovely melody:

It is *Love Confessed,* part of Walther's famous Prize Song, and is followed by a breathless phrase, *Impatient Ardor:*

There is a little interlude, when the woodwinds sound the *Master-singer Theme,* waspishly, as though making fun of the dignity of the masters, but after that the different motives combine to form a mighty climax.

ACT ONE. The curtains rise on the interior of Saint Katherine's Church. Young Walther von Stolzing is leaning against a column, trying to catch the attention of Eva, who is sitting in one of the last pews with Magdalene. Between the verses of the chorale the congregation is singing, the girl looks around shyly, and as the two exchange ardent glances the orchestra sounds the love themes heard in the prelude.

At last the service is over. Eva and Magdalene are among the last to leave, and, approaching them, the young man begs a word. Hastily, the girl sends her nurse to look for the kerchief and buckle she left in the pew. When they are alone, Walther turns to Eva eagerly.

"Forgive me," he cries, "but I must know one thing. Are you be-trothed?"

Before Eva can answer, Magdalene returns. Walther's question alarms the nurse, and she is trying to hurry her charge home when David appears and sets to work closing off the nave with curtains.

At once Magdalene is willing to linger, and tells Walther that Eva is to be the bride of the mastersinger who wins the song contest to be held the next day.

As he is not a mastersinger, Walther is much disturbed to hear this, but Eva reassures him. "It will be you or no one," she bursts out.

Shocked, Magdalene reminds the girl that she only met the young man the day before. While they are talking, David starts measuring with a chalk on a string.

"Whatever are up up to?" asks Magdalene, looking at him tenderly.

"Why, preparing for the masters," he answers. "They meet here today."

Magdalene is delighted. Walther must stay for the meeting, and while he is waiting David can teach him the rules of song-making. Joy-fully, the lovers plan to meet that evening, and the two women hurry off. Walther throws himself into a raised chair that the apprentices have dragged forward.

"Now begin!" David calls commandingly.

The knight is startled. "Begin?"

"Yes, that is what the Marker will say," David tells him, and lists all the things required of a master song—the right number of verses, the correct rhymes, the proper tones, until poor Walther's head is in a whirl.

Meanwhile the other apprentices have been busy assembling a small platform with curtains hanging about it. "This is where the Marker will sit and note down your mistakes," David tells the knight. "You are only allowed seven, so be careful. And now good luck!"

Joining hands, the apprentices dance around the Marker's stage. Suddenly they scatter.

Veit Pogner enters the church, talking with Beckmesser.

"But if Eva may decide whether or not she will accept the winner, what is the use of all my skill?" complains the Town Clerk fretfully.

Pogner suggests that Beckmesser find out how Eva feels about him before entering the contest, and, as the clerk turns aside to ponder the possibility of serenading the girl that night, Walther steps forward.

"You are surprised to see me here, I know," he says to Pogner, "but let me assure you that what truly brought me to Nuremberg was the wish to become a mastersinger."

Pogner is overjoyed, and introduces the young man to other members of the Guild, which is now assembling. Last of all Hans Sachs enters. The roll is called by the master of ceremonies, Fritz Kothner, and the burghers seat themselves.

The first matter to discuss is the festival on the morrow in honor of Midsummer or *Saint John's Day.*

Pogner tells the gathering that he has been distressed by hearing the burghers everywhere called misers. "To prove that we love art more than wealth," he declares, "I have decided to offer as prize to the winner of the contest, all my goods and—if she will accept him—the hand of my daughter, Eva."

The burghers congratulate Pogner on his generosity, but they are disturbed at the thought of allowing a maiden the freedom to refuse a mastersinger. Hans Sachs, who has none of the stuffy pride of the others, suggests that they let Eva and the people choose the winner.

"Once a year," he urges, as the masters rise in protest, "it would surely be wise to test our rules by popular vote, for only so can we keep our art fresh and true."

The apprentices clap their hands in delight, but the burghers are unwilling to give up any privileges.

"Can a widower try for the prize?" asks Beckmesser. "How about Sachs?"

"You and I are far too old to woo little Eva," replies the cobbler good-naturedly, much to the fury of the Town Clerk.

At this point Pogner introduces Walther. Beckmesser glares angrily at the young man, in whom he senses a dangerous rival, and, a little uneasy at the idea of a nobleman applying for membership in their Guild, the masters question Walther about his training.

The young man tells them that he learned of art from an ancient book written by the famous minstrel, Sir Walter von der Vogelweid.

"He has been dead a long time," remarks Beckmesser scornfully, but, undaunted, Walther declares himself ready to sing a trial song.

The Town Clerk goes to the Marker's platform with malicious satisfaction, and, warning that only seven mistakes are allowed, yanks the curtains shut. Kothner reads the rules and directs Walther to the raised singer's stool.

"Now begin!" calls the Marker loudly.

Musing, Walther repeats the words. "Now begin! So Spring cries through the land, and joyfully wood and glen reply." The harsh scratch of chalk is heard from the Marker's box. After a moment of hesitation, Walther continues. "Envious old Winter plots to destroy the Spring," he cries, looking in the direction of Beckmesser. "But now begin! My heart heard the command, and, awakening from its sleep, raised a glorious song of love."

Beckmesser tears open the curtains. "Are you finally finished?" he asks, showing the slate all covered with chalk marks. The masters burst out laughing, and are about to reject the young man when Sachs interrupts.

"I find this song clear and true, even though it does not agree with our rules," he declares. "Our good

*Hardly has Beckmesser sung a line when
the hammer comes down with a crash.*

Marker has allowed his wooing to influence him in judging his rival."

"So!" snarls Beckmesser. "If you would pay more attention to shoes and less to poetry, my fine cobbler, we would all be better served."

"You have me there," answers Sachs, laughing. But he urges Walther to go on with his song, and, raising his voice above the clamor of the burghers, the knight makes a last desperate effort.

"High over croaking magpies soars a golden bird," he sings. "I shall follow him to the source of true art where master-ravens cannot rise, and there sing my lady's praises."

With a gesture of contempt Walther strides from the hall, and, talking excitedly, the masters follow. Only Sachs is left, deep in thought.

ACT TWO. A winding lane separates the imposing residence of Veit Pogner from the house of Sachs. It is Saint John's Eve, and the apprentices are busy closing the shutters for the night. Magdalene slips out of Pogner's house, a basket on her arm. "Psst, David," she whispers. "See what I've brought you. . . . But first tell me, was Sir Walther made a mastersinger?"

David admits that the knight was rejected, and in alarm Magdalene hurries back, leaving David to the mercies of the other boys, who tease him about his sweetheart. A fight is just about to begin when Sachs appears and orders David inside.

As the cobbler follows his apprentice, Pogner and Eva return from a walk, talking about the festival on the morrow. Magdalene calls them in to supper. She whispers to the girl that Walther has been defeated, and in despair Eva decides to slip away later and ask Sachs to help her.

Night has now fallen. David carries his master's bench outside, then goes off to bed, leaving the cobbler to work by lamplight. The night air is fragrant with the scent of elder blossoms.

Pausing, Sachs muses on the song he heard that day. "No rules could possibly fit such a master work," he reflects. "Even if the others do not agree, Hans Sachs is well pleased with the singer." He sets to work cheerfully.

"Good evening, master."

Sachs turns in surprise. Eva has stolen from her house, and, attempting to hide her interest, she asks about the trial that morning. Sachs soon discovers that she is in love with Walther, but he wishes to test her, and pretends to dislike the knight. "How could we possibly approve of a man who is so much cleverer than we are?" he asks. "Why, he put us all to shame."

Eva leaves him angrily, and the shoemaker retires to his shop.

"Beckmesser is coming to serenade you tonight," whispers Magdalene.

"O, do take my bonnet and stand in the window in my place," Eva begs, looking anxiously up the street for Walther. At that moment the young man turns the corner, and with a cry of joy Eva rushes into his arms.

"Come away with me," he implores her passionately. "In my own house I am master; here there is no hope." A loud harsh sound is heard, and Walther grasps his sword wildly.

"Hush, beloved. It is the night watchman's horn." Telling him to hide, she slips into the house. The night watchman goes by slowly. "Ten o'clock," he calls. "Put out your lights and praise the Lord."

Eva returns dressed as Magdalene, but, as the lovers turn to flee, Sachs flings open his shutter and a broad beam of light falls across their path. They draw back hastily.

Unnoticed, Beckmesser has approached down the alley at the back, and now, pausing opposite Pogner's house, he tunes his lute noisily. At once Sachs withdraws his light. The Town Clerk strikes up a tinkling accompaniment, but as he is about to sing, there comes the resounding smack of hammer on leather and the shoemaker, who has brought his workbench outside again, bursts forth with a lusty ballad.

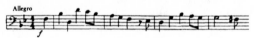

Whirling, Beckmesser rushes up to Sachs. "Up so late, master?" he sputters angrily.

"Yes, I'm finishing your shoes," answers the cobbler, pleasantly. "You see, I've taken your reproof in the Singing School to heart."

"That was only a joke," cries Beckmesser hastily, as the shoemaker lifts his hammer to begin again. "Master Sachs, I know your worth as a critic; pray listen to my little song and tell me what you find wrong with it."

Sachs agrees, provided he may get on with his work and hammer whenever he hears a fault. Magdalene now appears in the window dressed as Eva, and, making her a bow, Beckmesser begins:

But hardly has he sung a line when the hammer comes down with a crash. The clerk glares angrily. Sachs strikes again, then again, and, shaking his fist in a rage, Beckmesser raises his voice to a shriek, trying to drown out the din of the hammer.

David looks out of the window of Sachs' house. Why, that is Magdalene in the window opposite! And the Town Clerk down below serenading her! Rushing to the street, the boy falls upon Beckmesser. At once people gather at every window; others swarm into the lane in their nightdresses, hitting and pounding, and in a moment the fight becomes a free-for-all.

Suddenly the harsh bellow of the watchman's horn sounds above the turmoil. Panic-stricken, the people scatter in every direction. Sachs hustles Eva into the arms of her father, sends David into the shop with a kick, and drags in Walther after him. Only Beckmesser is left, and, still striking out blindly, he stumbles away into the night. Hardly has he vanished when the watchman appears. He stares at the empty streets in astonishment, then, chanting his call in a frightened voice, goes timidly up the lane. The full moon rises above the house-tops and floods the quiet streets with light.

ACT THREE, *Scene One.* The introduction to this act is like a musical description of Sachs. The cobbler-poet has long loved little Eva, and now, on the eve of her wedding, he knows he must renounce her at last. A beautiful, pensive melody, the theme of *Renunciation* begins the prelude:

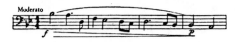

It merges into the *Chorale of Sachs:*

This is a grand and solemn hymn which will appear again when the people of Nuremberg greet the cobbler; this is, in turn, followed by sad echoes of the shoemaker's ballad. As the motive of *Renunciation* returns, the curtain rises on Sachs' workshop.

The master sits quietly reading in a large armchair. Presently David slips in, a basket on his arm. He sets it on the floor, and is looking at the contents when Sachs turns a page noisily. "Forgive me, master," cries the boy, startled. "If you only knew Magdalene as I do, then you would see why I beat up the clerk."

At last Sachs rouses himself from his reverie, and, turning to David, asks him to sing his verses for Saint John's Day.

"A lady from Nuremberg took her son to be baptized by Saint John in the Jordan," sings the boy. "But after she got home, she found his name had changed from Johannes to Hans . . . Hans! Why, today is your name-day, master." He offers Sachs his basket, but the cobbler shakes his head gently.

"Keep it yourself, lad, and now go dress for the festival." David scampers off.

"How mad the world is!" Sachs ponders. "In vain one looks for some reason why men fight each other so fiercely." He looks out the window at quaint, medieval Nuremberg, lying peacefully in the sunshine. "Was it a glowworm that started all the strife last night? A shoemaker, trying to prevent an elopement, woke the good folks, and lo, everybody fell to fighting. Well, we shall see if Sachs can guide this madness to a nobler end." Walther comes from the inner room, aglow from a dream he has had. Sachs urges him to tell it; perhaps it might be shaped into a mastersong.

"How would it be possible to create a song that is beautiful and is a mastersong as well?" the young man bursts out.

"My friend," says Sachs softly, "in youth many have the gift of song, but it is the spring that sings for them. Later, when the cares of life weigh one down, then he who can still shape a lovely melody is indeed a master."

Walther is confused by the many rules.

"Think only of your dream." Sachs responds, and after a moment's thought the young man begins.

"Morning was gleaming with rosy light," he sings softly.

He tells how in a garden he discovered a woman so lovely that her like was not to be found on earth. Sachs, who has jotted down the words, is much moved, and urges him to continue. But Walther rises impatiently—the rest must wait.

"Then let us dress for the festival," cries the cobbler.

Scarcely are they gone when Beckmesser limps in, gaily decked in his holiday clothes, but bruised and sore from his fight with David. He looks around suspiciously. Nobody is in sight. Still he is uneasy, and whirls quickly to see if anybody is behind him. At last, breathless, he leans against the table. Before him is a page of writing. "So!" he bursts out. "A trial song by Sachs!" Hearing someone coming, he hastily stuffs the sheet in his pocket.

Entering, Sachs wishes his visitor a happy wedding day.

"Don't try to fool me any more, cobbler," snarls Beckmesser in a rage. "I see through your plan. You want Eva yourself, and had me beaten last night so you could win the contest."

"You are mistaken, friend," answers the shoemaker quietly. "Courtship has never entered my mind."

Beckmesser pulls the paper from his pocket. "Is this your writing?"

"Certainly, and to save you from being a thief, I give you the poem."

"A poem by Sachs!" Beckmesser springs up in joyful surprise. "But wait. Is it a trap? Swear you will never claim the song as your own."

Smiling, Sachs promises, and the clerk rushes out gleefully. As he disappears down the street, Eva comes in. She is dressed in festal blue and white, but her face is sad.

"My shoe is too wide," she says, explaining her visit. "No, it pinches at the toe." As Sachs bends down to look, the chamber door opens and Walther stands on the threshold. Eva utters a cry of joy.

"Aha!" exclaims Sachs. "Now I see what is wrong with the shoe."

He takes it to his bench and pretends to work. "Today I heard a lovely song. If only someone would sing the final verse."

Joyously, Walther sings the closing stanzas of the Prize Song, and Eva listens, spellbound. As he finishes she suddenly bursts into tears. "O, Sachs," she sobs, throwing herself into the cobbler's arms. "I owe you everything, and if my choice were free, you alone would be my husband. But now my heart is mine no longer. . . ."

Deeply moved, the cobbler turns away for a moment. "My child," he says gently, while the orchestra whispers love themes from *Tristan und Isolde*, "I know Tristan's sad story too well to play the part of King Marke." He joins the hands of the lovers. "Let the right man claim his bride."

Magdalene arrives, and David runs to meet her. "Sir Walther's new song must be christened." Sachs announces solemnly. "But, since an apprentice cannot serve as a witness, I here and now make David a journeyman." He gives the young man a box on the ear. "The name of the song shall be 'The Morning Dream,' " the cobbler continues. "Now the godmother shall speak."

Flushed with joy, Eva tells of her new-found happiness,

and one by one the others add their voices, each speaking of what he hopes the day shall bring for him.

At last Sachs interrupts. "Come, it is time to be off." As the curtain falls trumpets sound a fanfare in the distance; all Nuremberg is gathering in the meadow beyond the city walls.

Scene Two. Merrymaking crowds throng the festival grounds. At one side stands a platform for the judges, and as the guilds arrive they plant their banners behind it. First come the shoemakers, then the tailors, and the bakers. A crowd of boys and girls start to dance. But from the river bank comes a shout: "The Mastersingers!" and the people make way respectfully as Kothner enters, waving the banner of the Masters' Guild. After him walk the other burghers and Eva.

Sachs rises to open the festivities, but of a sudden the people rush forward impulsively. Every head is bared, every face upturned, and in a mighty chorus the people raise their voices in love and praise to the cobbler-poet *(Chorale of Sachs)*. Almost overcome with emotion, he thanks them.

Then Kothner calls on Beckmesser to sing his song, and ribboned ushers lead the Town Clerk to a small grassy mound.

He tries to calm his uneasiness with a long prelude on the lute. At last he begins. "In the morning I shone with a rosy glow—with blood and scent," he quavers uncertainly, in his nervousness twisting the words all around. The people titter, and anxiously Beckmesser takes a hurried look at the poem in his pocket. But the further he goes the more mixed up he gets. Finally the crowd breaks into mocking laughter, and in a rage he rushes to the judges' stand.

"It was your beloved Sachs that wrote the trash," he shrieks, flinging the poem at the cobbler's feet, and storms away.

"This song is not by me," Sachs says quietly. "But he who wrote it, Sir Walther von Stolzing, will show you how it should really sound."

The young knight comes forward with firm step. Then, as all listen in breathless excitement, he sings his beautiful Prize Song.

People and masters alike unite in admiration. "Grant him the prize," they cry, and Eva lays a wreath of laurel on the young man's head.

Pogner comes forward to place the golden chain of the mastersingers about Walther's neck. The knight starts back impetuously. "No!" he exclaims. "Let me stay away from the masters!"

Shocked, and not knowing what to do, all look at Sachs. The old master is deeply hurt.

"Do not belittle the mastersingers," he says gravely. "For what you have won today as poet and singer, your sword and birth could never have gained for you." Walther grasps the cobbler's hand gratefully, and bows his head to receive the masters' chain.

"Honor the mastersinger!" shout the people, echoing the shoemaker's words. Eva and Walther whisper together for a moment. Then taking the wreath from her lover's head, Eva crowns Sachs with the laurel. The people burst into wild cheers. "Hail Sachs!" they cry, waving their kerchiefs and tossing their caps in the air. "Hail, Nuremberg's beloved Sachs!"

Orfeo ed Euridice

BY CHRISTOPH WILLIBALD VON GLUCK

Libretto by Ranieri di Calzabigi

PRINCIPAL CHARACTERS *(in order of appearance):*

Orfeo (contralto), a handsome Greek youth, famed for his wonderful gifts as a minstrel.

Amor (soprano), the god of love.

Euridice (soprano), the beloved wife of Orfeo, who has recently died.

PLACE: Greece and the Nether World.   TIME: Legendary.

ACT ONE. The curtain rises on the tomb of Euridice. Youths and maidens cluster about, bewailing their grief and trying to comfort Orfeo, who stands, sunk in despair, at the entrance to the tomb. But the young man cannot listen to them. "Euridice!" he calls wildly. "Euridice!"

At last he turns to his friends. "Your lamentations only add to my grief," he tells them. "Come, let us honor her memory with flowers."

In silence, his companions lay offerings of garlands and incense upon the grave, the torches are extinguished as a token of mourning, and sorrowfully the young people depart. Orfeo stands alone among the heaped-up blossoms.

"O, my beloved!" he cries. "With every dawn, with every sunset I bewail your death. Shall I never have an answer?"

Drearily, the groves and valleys echo his lament. "Euridice! Ah, everywhere Nature whispers your sweet name. But you are gone, and I must live. . . . Merciless gods, demons of the underworld, I will snatch her from you. Yes, my lyre shall open a way for me, even to the gates of Hades—"

"Then go!" calls a high, clear voice. Orfeo turns in amazement. Before him, bathed in golden light, stands Amor. "Despair no longer," the god tells him, "but descend swiftly to Pluto's dark realm. If you can charm the guardians of the Nether World with your art, and are willing to obey the commands of Jupiter, you shall lead Euridice back to earth."

"Tell me what I must do," begs Orfeo joyfully. "I will obey."

"You are forbidden to look at your wife before reaching the earth," Amor replies. "One glance, and she shall be lost to you forever."

He gives Orfeo the golden lyre that he carries, and vanishes as suddenly as he came.

The young man looks after him with mixed emotions. "Euridice alive again!" he exults. "O, what joy! . . . But that cruel command. Ah, my beloved, what pain and sorrow it will cost you." Distant thunder is heard. Orfeo seizes his lyre. "The gods have spoken," he cries, his eyes flashing. "I shall succeed in spite of everything."

Amid lightning and thunder he hastens off in search of the path to Hades.

ACT TWO. Demons and furies crowd before the smoldering gates of Erebus. Above them rises a vast stairway, leading up through the gloom of the Nether World. Suddenly a lyre is heard. At once the cluster of creatures before the gates erupt into a mass of writhing limbs and bodies.

"What mortal dares invade our realm?" they scream. The mists at the upper reaches of the stairway part, and Orfeo stands before them.

"O Furies," he pleads, "have pity on me and let me pass."

"No!" they shriek, reaching up toward him with clutching fingers.

But the minstrel is undaunted. Drawing magical tones from his lyre, he tells them of the despair that fills his heart. "I have lost my beloved," he laments. "Ah, let my prayers move you to compassion."

At last even the souls of the damned are enthralled by the magic of Orfeo's singing. Their furious shouts die away to murmurs, and, wondering, they draw back as the young man descends into the abyss.

"Open the gates," they cry softly. "Let him enter the realm of death."

From below flames leap up, the Furies whirl in frenzied dance, but unafraid Orfeo passes through the fiery gates into the world beyond.

ACT THREE. Serene and beautiful, the Elysian fields stretch to the cloudless horizon. Bands of spirits dance in the clear, sparkling air.

One of their number sings of the joys of death. "Peace reigns in these groves and meadows," she exults. "Here all the sorrows of life are forgotten."

They wander away, and presently Orfeo appears. "What pure, clear light!" he exclaims, gazing about him in wonder. "What lovely meadows! Shall I find you here, my beloved?"

From the distance comes the sound of mysterious voices. "Orfeo," they call, "Euridice approaches."

Mindful of the command of the god, the young man shields his eyes, and, as the spirits return and weave about him gracefully, he holds out his hand, imploring them to bring her to him. At last a veiled figure is led forward. It is Euridice. But Orfeo dares not look at her. Striving to master the joy and anguish that fill his heart, the minstrel takes her gently by the hand. The long, fateful journey back to earth has begun.

ACT FOUR, *Scene One*. Still with his gaze averted, the minstrel leads his bride upward through the winding rocky passageways of the infernal regions. Euridice cannot understand why he will not look at her.

"Have I lost my beauty?" she asks sorrowfully. "Why do you turn away from me?"

Struggling against his longing to take her in his arms, Orfeo begs her to believe in him. "I love you," he cries.

"Then why are you so cruel?" she answers. "Is this the happiness you offer me on earth? Ah, take back your gift, betrayer. and let me return to the peace of Elysium."

Overcome with despair, the young man sweeps her into his arms. But even as he gazes at the face he loves so well, the pallor of death spreads across her features, and with a little sigh, she sinks suddenly at his feet.

"I have slain her," he gasps in horror. and tries frantically to revive her, sobbing her name over and over. "What shall I do without my Euridice? Where shall I go without my love?"

Then, rising, he draws a dagger from his belt. "I am still near the gates of death. I will come to you, my love. . . ." But, as he lifts the weapon, a dazzling light breaks through the gloom. Amor stands before him.

"Hold, Orfeo!" cries the god. "You have suffered enough. Euridice, awake." At the command, the maiden stirs. Life flows back into her limbs, and, rising from the ground, she rushes into the arms of her lover. In a transport of joy and gratitude, the minstrel dedicates himself forever to the praises of the god.

Scene Two. Towering high above a beautiful garden stands the temple of Amor. A crowd of youths and maidens have gathered there to await the coming of the god, and, as he approaches with Orfeo and Euridice. they burst into a hymn of praise. Bacchantes from the temple whirl in joyous dance.

Amor leads the reunited lovers up the great steps before the temple, and at the summit he crowns the faithful minstrel and his wife with garlands of flowers. "Hail, god of love," shout the people. "May you reign forever more!"

Pagliacci

(THE STROLLING PLAYERS)

BY RUGGIERO LEONCAVALLO

Libretto by the composer

PRINCIPAL CHARACTERS *(in order of appearance):*

Tonio (baritone), a deformed and bitter actor, member of a troupe of strolling players.

Canio (tenor), the violent and impulsive leader of the troupe.

Nedda (soprano), his young wife.

Peppe (tenor), a kindly actor.

Silvio (baritone), a young villager.

PLACE: A village in the province of Calabria, Italy.   TIME: About 1865.

THE PROLOGUE begins with an energetic theme, suggesting the melodrama and fantasy of play-acting:

Real sorrow sounds in the fragment of melody that follows:

It merges swiftly, though, into a graceful love theme:

The motive of the theater returns, and suddenly Tonio puts his head through the curtains. "Ladies and gentlemen," he calls, "will you allow me to introduce myself? I am the Prologue!" Advancing to the footlights, he announces that he has not come to assure the listeners that what they are about to see is only imaginary, but rather to tell them that the author is going to present the emotions of real men in his play. "Our hearts will speak to you," Tonio concludes, "for we are men like yourselves. . .

So let us begin. Ring up the curtain!"

ACT ONE. A crowd of villagers has gathered by the open-air theater on the outskirts of Montalto to greet the returning players. "There they come," shout the people as drums and cymbals sound down the road. Surrounded by whistling boys, the actors drive up in their donkey cart. Canio, the leader, bows and nods to the cheering mob. Then, standing up, he pounds his drum loudly for attention. "We shall give a performance tonight at seven," he announces. "Come one, come all, and honor us with your presence."

"We'll be there, never fear!" answers the crowd joyously as the actor jumps down from the cart.

Tonio shuffles over to help Nedda, but, turning quickly, Canio gives him a box on the ear. "Get away from there," he snaps. "I'll help her myself."

The people laugh. "Now you're put in your place, mister lover," they jeer at Tonio, and the clown limps off behind the theater, glaring angrily at his master.

A group of villagers gather around Canio. "Come, have a drink with us," they urge. The actor agrees gladly, and Peppe decides to go along, too.

"Are you coming, Tonio?" calls Canio.

"No. I'm tending to the donkey," the fellow calls gruffly from behind the theater.

"Aha," says one of the villagers with a wink. "He's planning to make love to Nedda while you're away, Pagliaccio."

"You think so?" answers Canio lightly, but his brow darkens. There is a pause. "It would be safer not to play that game with me," he continues. "For real life is very different from the stage. Up there—as Pagliaccio—if I find my lady with another man, I just give them a good

scolding. But if Nedda should ever be false to me in real life. . . ." His
eyes flash dangerously. Then he forces himself to be calm again. "Yes,
it would really be safer not to play that game with me, sir."

Surprised at his show of temper, the villagers try to restore him to
good humor, and, kissing his wife, Canio goes off with them to the
tavern. The church bells have begun to ring, and couples pass along
the road on their way to the service. At last Nedda is alone.

She looks after her husband anxiously. "His eyes frightened me,"
she murmurs. "Suppose he should discover my secret? Suppose he
should catch us. . . ? But enough of these horrid thoughts." She gazes
up at the summer sky. "How bright the sun is!" she sings. "And the
birds! Where can they be flying? Perhaps they are chasing a dream, too."

"I am the Prologue," says Tonio.

Tonio creeps from behind the theater. The girl hears his heavy breathing and turns sharply. "What are you doing here?"

"Your song brought me, Nedda," the man whines. "It was so beautiful."

"You talk like a poet!" she mocks.

"Don't laugh," Tonio pleads. "O, Nedda, I know I'm ugly and deformed, but I have a heart like other men, and I dream . . . I dream . . . let me tell you that. . . ."

"You love me," she interrupts scornfully. "Fool! Save that for the performance tonight when you'll be acting the part. . . . Come, be off, or I'll call Canio."

"Not till I've kissed you," he pants, trying to seize her. She snatches up a whip and slashes him across the face. Tonio reels back.

"You'll pay dearly for that, Nedda!" he screams.

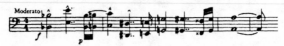

As he shuffles away behind the theater, the love theme heard in the prologue whispers in the orchestra, and a young man leaps over the wall at one side. "Nedda!" he calls softly. She turns, startled.

"O, Silvio, what a terrible risk to take, coming in the daytime. You just missed Tonio. He tried to kiss me, and I whipped him, the cur!"

Silvio sweeps her into his arms. "You must not live this kind of life any longer," he cries passionately. "Nedda, tomorrow your troupe will go away. O, if it is true that you have never loved Canio, then fly with me tonight."

She hesitates, torn between her love for him and her duty to her husband.

Tonio appears at the back. "The wanton!" he chokes, staring at Nedda in Silvio's arms, and the motive of vengeance mutters grimly as he steals off toward the tavern. But the lovers do not see him.

"Tell me you will come, Nedda," pleads Silvio, and at last she consents. Hastily they make their plans. "I'll be waiting for you at midnight," he whispers, letting himself over the wall. Tonio and Canio appear at the crossroads in back.

"*Till tonight, then—and forever I'll be yours!*" Nedda calls after her lover.

Canio hears and rushes forward with a shout of rage. The girl tries to bar his way, but he pushes her aside and leaps over the wall in a wild effort to catch the fleeing villager. But the man has vanished. "That shows how well he knows the path," pants Canio furiously, climbing back. "But no matter, you shall tell me his name!" He seizes Nedda roughly and draws his dagger. "Speak now, and be quick!"

"Never!"

"Then I'll—"

Dashing up, Peppe wrenches away the knife. "The folks are on their way to the performance, master," he pleads, holding back the struggling man. "Nedda, go dress yourself." The girl goes inside, and Peppe follows.

"Her lover will come back," Tonio whispers to Canio. "We'll catch him tonight. Now it's time to work." He goes after the others.

Canio stares at the stage in despair. "How can I act when my head's whirling with madness," he cries. "But I must, I must . . . for I'm not a man—I'm only a Pagliaccio!" He laughs bitterly. "Put on the grease paint, then, and the clown's smock.

What if Harlequin does take Columbine from you? The people pay and have to have their fun. . . ." Sobbing, he pushes through the curtains and disappears.

ACT TWO. Long wooden benches have been set up in front of the stage, and, taking his position at one side, Tonio pounds his drum to call the people to the performance. They stream in from all directions —women and children, peasants and villagers, all decked out in holiday clothes. Among them is Silvio.

At last the curtain goes up, and the audience applauds in delight as a little room is seen with Nedda, dressed as Columbine, seated at a table.

"Performance tonight at seven," calls Canio.

"My husband, Pagliaccio, won't be home till late," she announces with satisfaction. A guitar sounds off stage, and she rushes to the window.

Peppe, dressed as Harlequin, has come to serenade his loved one. "O, Columbine, open wide your window," he sings.

Hardly has he finished when Tonio, playing the part of Taddeo, peeps through the door. "Isn't she lovely!" he exclaims, sending the audience into gales of laughter with his comic gestures. Limping forward, he makes love to Columbine as he has done so often before in the play, but now his words have a double meaning. "O, I know you are good," he whines. "But why are you so cruel to me?"

Harlequin has climbed through the window and crept up behind the kneeling clown. Now he gives him a resounding kick. Taddeo retreats hastily, and his rival sits down to supper with the lady. But a moment later, the clown returns, trembling with mock fright. "Pagliaccio has returned," he stammers and runs to hide. Harlequin leaps out the window.

"*Till tonight, then—and forever I'll be yours!*" Columbine calls after him as Canio comes through the door, dressed as Pagliaccio. He staggers back on hearing the very same words that she had said to her lover. Then, pulling himself together, he tries to go on with the play. "There was a man here!" he declares harshly.

"What nonsense!"

"Then why is the table set for two?"

"It was Taddeo," cries Columbine, dragging out the cripple.

"O, do believe her, sir," Tonio sneers. "Those lovely lips could never lie." The audience gives a roar of delight, and, almost beside himself, Pagliaccio turns on the girl. "What is his name?" he shouts.

"Whose name, Pagliaccio?" she asks, still playing her part.

"No! I am Pagliaccio no longer," Canio cries wildly, tearing the clown's cap from his head. "I am the foolish man who saved you from hunger and poverty and gave you his love. . . ." He drops onto the chair, overcome with despair, and the people in the audience lean forward breathlessly. "What life-like acting," they whisper to one another.

"O, I was blind," Canio continues passionately.

"But now I know you for what you are. What is your lover's name?"

Nedda turns to Tonio. "Tell him the man who was sitting here was only harmless Harlequin," she pleads. The people burst out laughing, but they stop abruptly as Canio seizes the girl, his eyes blazing furiously. "You defy me, do you?" he shouts, and whips out his knife. "Who was it?"

"I'll never tell," Nedda shrieks, struggling to get away. The listeners rise to their feet. "Is it real?" they gasp. "Do you think they mean it?" Peppe climbs in the window in his Harlequin costume, but Tonio holds him back.

With a last desperate effort, Nedda wrenches away from Canio and flees toward the audience. He strikes her down. "Silvio!" she screams, and falls.

Tearing himself away from the villagers who have been holding him, the young man leaps to the stage. Canio plunges his knife into his rival's heart. Then—as if stupefied—he lets the dagger fall. "The comedy is ended!" he gasps.

Parsifal

BY RICHARD WAGNER

Libretto by the composer

PRINCIPAL CHARACTERS (*in order of appearance*):

Gurnemanz (bass), senior knight of the Grail.

Kundry (soprano), a wild woman of mysterious origin, who serves the brotherhood of the Grail.

Amfortas (baritone), the king of Montsalvat. Wounded in an encounter with Klingsor, enemy of the knights, he lives in pain, awaiting the rescuer promised him in a vision.

Parsifal (tenor), a strange, impetuous youth.

Klingsor (baritone), a magician who seeks to lure the knights to destruction in his magic garden.

PLACE: In and near the castle of Montsalvat, Spain.   TIME: Middle Ages.

THE PRELUDE begins with a wonderful melody which rises and falls mysteriously, symbolizing the *Eucharist,* or Last Supper of Our Lord:

There is a long silence, then the *Holy Grail* theme soars upward, as though reaching to Heaven itself:

It is followed by the ringing notes of *Faith:*

The *Eucharist* theme returns, this time over a surging tremolo, and last of all come three strident notes, part *A* of the *Eucharist* motive:

They symbolize the *Sacred Lance* that once pierced the Saviour's side, and which has been stolen from Montsalvat. ,

ACT ONE. *Scene One.* The curtain rises on a forest glade near the castle. Gurnemanz is sleeping under a towering tree, while beyond, the blue crags at the far side of a narrow lake glimmer in the early morning light. A distant call sounds.

"Awake, children," cries Gurnemanz, arousing two squires who slumber at his feet. "Let us give thanks to God."

As they arise from their devotions, two knights arrive from the castle on their way to the lake to prepare the king's morning bath. Gurnemanz questions them eagerly. How does the king feel after using the wild herb that one of the brotherhood won for him?

"Alas, the pain returned more violently than ever."

Sorrowfully, Gurnemanz admits that all their hopes are futile. Amfortas must wait for the Chosen One who has been promised to cure him. "And who is he?" ask the knights.

At that moment the squires break in excitedly: "Look, there comes the wild rider, Kundry!"

A weird creature, dressed in rags, staggers in. Her black hair flies in wild disorder about the dark, distorted face, her piercing eyes are fixed and staring. "Here, balsam," she gasps, thrusting a small vial into Gurnemanz's hand. "If this does not ease the king's pain, all Arabia has nothing more to offer." Turning aside, she flings herself on the ground like an animal, refusing to speak further.

· A procession of knights and squires winds down the hill, bearing Amfortas. As they reach the glade, the attendants set down the litter. The sick man raises himself weakly on his elbow and gazes about at the beauty of the woods.

"All this effort is in vain," he cries despairingly. "No one can cure me but the Promised One, and surely his name is Death."

Gurnemanz urges him to try the salve Kundry has brought, and the procession moves off toward the lake.

Some of the squires turn on Kundry. "Why do you lie there like a wild beast?" they taunt.

Quickly Gurnemanz intervenes. "Has she ever harmed you?" he asks.

"No, but she hates us. She is a sorceress!"

Gurnemanz admits that misfortune always overtakes the brotherhood when Kundry is long away. He turns to her. "Where were you, Kundry, on that fateful day when Amfortas lost the Sacred Lance?"

The creature crouching at his feet does not answer.

"If she is so helpful," urges a squire, "why not send her after the Lance?"

"That is reserved for another," responds Gurnemanz gloomily, and he tells them the mournful story of Amfortas' downfall. Long years ago, Titurel, the founder of their order, built the sanctuary to guard the Holy Grail and Sacred Lance. Only the pure in heart might serve the Grail, and so when the magician, Klingsor, aspired to join the fellowship he was rejected. In revenge he conjured a magic garden out of the desert, and there lovely women wait to lure the knights to their destruction.

At length Amfortas succeeded his aged father, Titurel. as king. Ambitious to overthrow the magician. the young man took the Sacred Lance with him against the foe. But in the magic garden he was bewitched by a beautiful woman, and Klingsor, snatching away the Lance, dealt him a fearful wound. This wound has never healed. In despair, Amfortas prayed for help, and a mysterious voice bade him "await the Chosen One, a guileless fool made wise through pity."

The squires repeat the prophecy softly, but their words are interrupted by shouts from the lakeside. A wounded swan circles overhead, then falls crashing into the shrubbery.

"Who did this bloody deed?" cries Gurnemanz in horror.

"Here is the culprit!" The knights have crowded up from the lake, and now thrust forward a strange, awkward youth.

The boy admits his crime gleefully. "Yes. I shot the swan. I shoot everything that flies."

"How could you murder in the peace of this forest?" asks Gurnemanz reproachfully. He takes the youth by the hand and draws him close to the swan. "See how your shaft has pierced him. Look at the beautiful plumage all stained with blood. the staring eyes, the drooping wings."

Overcome with shame, the boy flings away his bow and arrows. Gurnemanz looks at him more kindly.

"What is your name, lad?"

"I don't know." replies the boy.

Gurnemanz tries again. but the youth can answer none of his questions, and at last, turning to his fellows, the knight bids them return to the king.

When they have gone. the boy speaks. "I have a mother." he says. "Her name is Broken-heart, and we lived alone on the edge of a forest."

Kundry has been listening with interest. "His father, Gamuret, was slain in battle," she calls out suddenly. "His mother hoped to save him from a like fate and raised him as a fool." She laughs harshly.

"Yes," cries the youth eagerly. "And once I saw a band of riders in glittering armor. I ran after them, but they left me far behind. Since then I have been fighting my way through the world."

"But your mother—she must grieve for you."

"His mother grieves no more," cries Kundry shrilly. "I rode by on my journey and saw her die. She asked me to greet you, fool!"

"Dead! My mother!" In a rage the boy springs at her, and Gurnemanz drags him off with difficulty.

"What has she done to you?" he asks. "She spoke the truth, for Kundry never lies."

The boy turns pale. Gurnemanz helps him to a rocky seat and Kundry hastily fetches water from a nearby spring to revive him. The knight commends her act of mercy, but she turns away gloomily.

A great weariness has come over Kundry, and animal-like she longs to creep into the woods and hide herself. Suddenly she starts back in fear. "No! Not slumber!" The sinister motives of *Enchantment:*

and *Klingsor:*

sound in the orchestra, weighing her down as though with magic fetters. "The call has come," she mutters despairingly. "I must go. . . ."

As she stumbles out of sight, the knights bearing the king return from the lake and go toward the castle. Gurnemanz follows them at a distance with the boy, whose strange history has interested him. Indeed, he wonders if this may not be the guileless fool, come at last to rescue Amfortas.

They disappear in the woods, and the curtain closes, but the orchestra describes their journey up through the rocky passes to the temple on the lofty heights. From the distance comes the sound of tolling bells,

echoing the footsteps of the climbing men. Then, suddenly a wild lament bursts from the orchestra, as though the suffering king, Amfortas, were lifting his voice in a *Cry to the Saviour:*

The curtains part on the mighty hall of the Grail castle.

Scene Two. Gurnemanz leaves the boy standing at one side and goes to meet the king, who is borne in on his litter. As Amfortas takes his place, the voice of Titurel is heard from the tomb-like vault where the aged king lies, too feeble to join the brotherhood in their service.

"Uncover the Grail!"

"No!" Amfortas stops the squires. "O, may none of you ever feel the anguish awakened in me, the only sinner amongst you, when I see the Holy Cup that gives you such joy." In despair he begs Heaven for mercy. "Take away my kingship," he pleads. "Only let me die."

In answer, mysterious voices whisper the words of the prophecy: "Await the guileless fool. . . ."

Again Titurel commands the unveiling of the Grail, and, as the attendants uncover a marvelous crystal cup, all kneel in prayer. Darkness descends upon the hall. Suddenly a dazzling ray of light falls from above. The chalice gleams blood-red, and in ecstasy Amfortas waves it gently to and fro, blessing the bread and wine held up by the kneeling servants. At last the glow fades. The cup is returned to its shrine, and when the brotherhood has finished its repast the knights depart, bearing away Amfortas, whose wound has broken out afresh.

All this time the strange youth has been watching silently. When Amfortas cried out in agony, he pressed his hand upon his heart, but he has not moved. Gurnemanz shakes him by the arm. "Did you understand what you saw?"

"Now let Gurnemanz proclaim me ruler of the Grail."

The boy shakes his head, and angrily the knight drives him from the temple. But as Gurnemanz turns to follow his companions, a voice from the heights above softly repeats the promise: "Await the Chosen One, a guileless fool made wise through pity!"

ACT TWO, *Scene One*. Introduced by the sinister motive of *Klingsor*, which storms furiously through the orchestra, and the chromatic phrase of *Enchantment,* the second act opens on a tower in the magician's castle. Battlements jut up blackly against a lurid green sky.

Within, Klingsor bends over a magic crystal. "The time is at hand," he mutters. "Hither, Kundry!"

A blue light appears in the darkness below. and silently Kundry rises from the depths. She is wrapped in veils, her face is deathly white. Suddenly she wakes with a shriek that dies away in a wail of misery.

"Have you been serving the knights again?" taunts her master. "They treat you like a dog, but here, where even Amfortas once fell a victim to your enchantment, you fare much better. Today, you shall conquer the most dangerous foe of all—a youth shielded by foolishness."

"I will not," gasps Kundry hoarsely. "You cannot force me."

But the magician's will is the stronger. As he rises to summon his vassals to fight the approaching enemy, she bursts into wild laughter, then sinks, shrieking, into the abyss. Klingsor turns. "Kundry!" he calls. "What, already at work?" He waves his hand, and the tower vanishes. In its place rises a magic garden.

Scene Two. The youth who killed the swan stands upon the low rampart at the back. He has defeated the magician's knights, and now, as he gazes about him in astonishment, flower maidens rush upon him from every side. At first they are angry because he has wounded their sweethearts, but when he tells them he has come to play with them, they are overjoyed. "Come, gentle lover," they sing tenderly, each trying to embrace him.

Suddenly a voice of marvelous beauty rises above the clamor. "Parsi-fal!"

"Parsifal!" whispers the boy. "My mother once called me that." He turns fearfully. There, on a flowery couch, reclines a woman so lovely that for a moment he is speechless. It is Kundry. She sends the flower maidens away, and, beckoning the youth to her side, gently tells him how his mother died of a broken heart, waiting for him to return to her.

"O, what have I done?" the boy cries, overcome with sorrow, and sinks to the ground at Kundry's feet. She bends over him tenderly.

"Acknowledge your guilt and grieve no more," she whispers. "Through me your mother sends you her last blessing in a kiss." Twin-ing her arms about his neck, the enchantress presses her lips to his.

Parsifal starts up with a cry of anguish. "Amfortas! The spear-wound!" He presses his hands against his heart as though to subdue some fearful pain. "Now I understand what I saw in the temple. Now I understand the voice that cried to me to rescue the sanctuary from guilty hands."

Kundry has watched him in fear and wonder. "If you are the Deliv-erer," she pleads, "have pity on *me*." She tells him the tragic story of her life. "I saw the Lord on His way to the Cross . . . and *laughed*. His glance fell on me. . . . Now I seek Him from age to age. But whenever I feel that He is near, my accursed laughter re-turns—yet another sinner falls victim to my en-chantment." Parsifal turns from her in horror. "Be mine for only one hour," she implores, trying to embrace him. "Then I will be re-deemed at last."

He repulses her violently. "Show me the way to Amfortas and you shall be saved."

"Never!" Wild with fury, she summons Kling-sor to her aid, and the magician appears on the rampart, armed with the Sacred Lance. He hurls it at Parsifal. But the youth catches it in mid-air. "Thus I destroy your enchantment," he cries, swinging the spear in the sign of the

Cross, and as if by magic the castle crumbles into ruins, the garden fades into a desert.

Climbing the shattered walls, Parsifal looks back to where Kundry lies prostrate on the ground. "You may yet be redeemed through faith," he calls, as he sets out in search of Amfortas.

ACT THREE. *Scene One.* The prelude begins mournfully with a slow, brooding melody, that suggests the dreary wastes of the *Desert:*

Later, the *Grail* motive appears, but it sweeps up the scale with a harsh and discordant ring, as though calamity had befallen the knights, its guardians. Then follows the strident motive of the *Lance,* and with it, strangely distorted, that of *Promise.*

At last the curtain rises. It is early morning and sunlight lies on the flowery meadows that stretch from a little grove off to the snow-capped mountains in the distance. Years have passed. From a hermit's hut at one side comes Gurnemanz, now very old; he goes to investigate a dull groaning that comes from a near-by thicket.

"Kundry! You again!" Dragging her to the spring he attempts to revive her. Suddenly she utters a cry and staggers to her feet. The wild, haunted look of earlier days is gone, her pale face has become almost ethereal, and, bending before him, she begs brokenly to be allowed to serve.

Gurnemanz is amazed. But as he ponders on the change in her, she points out a figure approaching through the woods. It is a knight, clad in dark armor, and bearing a spear in his hand.

The old man tells his strange guest that he is in the domain of the Grail, where no man may carry weapons. In response the knight thrusts his spear upright in the earth. Laying his helm and sword before it, he kneels in prayer. It is the youth whom Gurnemanz drove from the sanctuary so long ago.

At last Parsifal rises. "Have I really found you?" he asks, turning to

Gurnemanz. "Ah, the way has been long." He describes his wanderings. "An evil curse hid the path from me," he declares. "Again and again I was wounded in guarding the precious weapon that I dared not use in battle. But see! Before you, gleaming and undefiled, is the Sacred Lance of the Grail."

Deeply moved, the old knight gives thanks to Heaven. "The brotherhood needs you desperately," he tells Parsifal. "Since the day when you were here, Amfortas has refused to uncover the Grail, and, deprived of its light, the knights have lost their strength, while our beloved Titurel has died."

Parsifal is in despair. "O, why did I not return sooner?" he cries wildly. "How shall I atone for my guilt?" He sinks, fainting, to the ground.

Gurnemanz revives him with water from the holy spring; Kundry bathes and anoints his feet, drying them with her long black hair. As she works, the young man gazes at her quietly. "You have washed my feet," he says gently. "Now let Gurnemanz anoint my head and proclaim me ruler of the Grail."

The old man lays his hands on Parsifal's head in blessing.

As he finishes, the new king dips his hand in the holy well and baptizes the kneeling woman before him. "Be absolved," he whispers. "Believe in the Redeemer!" She sinks weeping to the ground.

Parsifal gazes about him in wonder at the fresh beauty of nature.

"It is *the Magic of Good Friday*," Gurnemanz explains:

"Alas!" cries Parsifal. "Today all the world must weep in mourning."

"Not so!" the old man replies. "Today nature rejoices in the Saviour's love, for on Good Friday He died that we might live."

The tolling of bells is heard in the distance. "Come," says the aged knight. "It is the funeral of my lord, Titurel." Holding the Sacred Lance aloft, Parsifal goes with Gurnemanz toward the castle. Kundry follows silently. As they disappear, the curtain falls, but again the music describes the slow ascent, gradually swelling to a massive funeral chant against which the bells toll louder and louder. The curtains part on the Grail hall.

Scene Two. Chanting mournfully, the knights bear in the black-draped coffin of Titurel and the litter of the wretched king, come to officiate at the last rites of his father.

"Who killed our founder? Who withheld the light of the Grail from him?" cry the knights. "There he comes, the unworthy guardian."

Brokenly, Amfortas kneels beside the bier. "You who are already before the throne of Heaven," he pleads, "pray that I may die."

"Reveal the Grail!" shout the knights, pressing about him. Amfortas staggers to his feet in despair.

"Never! With death at hand, shall I turn back to life?" He tears open his vestment. "Here is the wound. Plunge in your swords, you heroes. Slay the sinner."

Unnoticed, Parsifal has entered the hall. "Only the weapon that pierced you can end your sufferings," he cries, touching the breast of the frantic king with the Lance. Amfortas' face lights up with sudden joy. He lifts his hands in adoration to the Lance, whose point glows blood-red.

Parsifal places the spear on the altar and sinks in prayer before the Grail. Darkness envelopes the sanctuary. Then, once again, light falls from above. As the new king waves the chalice in blessing, a dark figure reaches up toward its radiance. It is Kundry. The light of the Grail falls upon her, and slowly she sinks down, freed at last from her age-long pilgrimage.

Suddenly a white dove descends from the heights above. Fluttering, it hovers over Parsifal—the brotherhood of Montsalvat has been redeemed by the guileless fool.

THE RING OF THE NIBELUNG

A Tragic Tale of Gods and Heroes in Three Dramas and a Prologue

BY RICHARD WAGNER

Librettos by the composer

PLACE: Rhine country and legendary habitation of the gods.   TIME: Legendary.

THE PROLOGUE:

Rheingold

PRINCIPAL CHARACTERS *(in order of appearance)*:

Woglinde (soprano)
Wellgunde (mezzo-soprano) } three lovely watermaidens, who keep watch over the golden treasure that lies at the bottom of the Rhine.
Flosshilde (contralto)

Alberich (baritone), the Nibelung, an evil, misshapen dwarf from the caverns of Nibelheim, deep in the earth.

Fricka (mezzo-soprano), the goddess of marriage, and the wife of Wotan.

Wotan (bass-baritone). haughty and ambitious ruler of the gods.

Freia (soprano), goddess of love, and keeper of the golden apples.

Fasolt (bass), a kind-hearted but stupid giant.

Fafner (bass). his crafty, vicious brother.

Froh (tenor), god of spring and youth.

Donner (baritone), god of thunder.

Loge (tenor), the cunning god of fire.

Mime (tenor), whining, cringing brother of Alberich, the Nibelung.

Erda (contralto), mysterious goddess of the earth.

Prelude. From the orchestra comes a deep sound that rises slowly upward, flowing and surging on like the swift current of a mighty river:

Gradually it subsides into the murmur of waves, and the curtain rises on the green, twilit depths of the Rhine.

ACT ONE, *Scene One.* "Weia, Waga, wandering waters," calls a clear voice:

Woglinde swims gracefully through the flood, followed by Wellgunde and Flosshilde, who dive after her with merry cries.

On the river bed below crouches Alberich.

"You above there!" he cries hoarsely. "How you delight me! For you I would gladly leave Nibelheim."

Startled, the nixies dive closer.

"Why, the gnome is in love!" they exclaim. Woglinde beckons Alberich. He clambers eagerly over the slippery rocks; as he reaches her side, she darts away. Wellgunde and Flosshilde call to him. They, too, slip from the dwarf's embraces, and wild with rage he pursues them from rock to rock. At last he sinks down, exhausted.

Suddenly the swaying waters are lit by a magical glow that streams from the summit of a great rock which juts up out of the depths, and a mysterious call sounds in the orchestra:

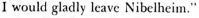

"Look, sisters," cries Woglinde, "the Rhinegold wakes from his sleep!" In wild joy the three swim about the rock, chanting a hymn of praise:

Alberich stares at the glittering peak. "What is it?" he whispers.

"Where do you come from, never to have heard of the Rhinegold?" retort the maidens. "Why, all the world knows of its wonderful powers."

"He who forged it into a ring would become master of the world," Wellgunde adds. In alarm, Flosshilde begs her to be careful lest the dwarf steal their treasure. But the others laugh at her.

"Only he who renounces love can make a ring of the gold," they reply. "And no man will give up love—least of all this foolish gnome."

Alberich has listened closely to their talk. "Love is denied me," he mutters. "Well, then, I shall have power!" Springing to the rock, he clambers furiously to the top.

"Hear me, you floods!" he screams, reaching out his hand for the treasure. "I renounce love forever!" With a fearful wrench he tears the gold from the rock, and plunges downward.

Blackness engulfs the Rhine. The maidens dive after the thief, screaming for help, but as they plunge into the murky depths the flood seems to sink with them, changing gradually into dark and swirling clouds. The motive of the *Ring* sounds, as though the Nibelung were already at work, shaping the fateful charm.

Then the clouds grow lighter, the mists clear away, and a mountain height appears.

Scene Two. Wotan and Fricka lie asleep on a flowery bank. Behind them the sun glitters on the turrets of Valhalla, towering loftily on a crag at the far side of a gorge.

As Fricka awakens, her gaze falls on the castle, and she calls to her husband in alarm. The god looks up at the mighty pile.

"At last it is finished!" he exclaims proudly. "I greet you, eternal home of the gods!"

"Yes," answers Fricka bitterly, "but have you forgotten that Freia is pledged to the giants in payment for building it?"

"Don't worry," says Wotan. "I don't intend to give up Freia." Even as he speaks, the maiden enters in wild flight. Wotan asks her if she has seen Loge. It was the god of fire who persuaded him to make the agreement with the giants, promising to find a fitting ransom for Freia. But Loge is nowhere to be seen, and, striding down the slope, the two giants confront Wotan.

"Your castle is finished," declares Fasolt. "We have come to fetch Freia—our promised reward."

"Surely you did not take seriously what was spoken in jest," Wotan replies lightly. "Ask something else, friend. I cannot give you Freia."

For a moment Fasolt is speechless with astonishment. "So!" he shouts angrily. "We toil day and night to win the goddess that she may brighten our dull lives, and now you tell us the treaty was a joke. . . ."

Fafner draws him aside roughly. "Stop your stupid chatter," he snarls. "Freia's beauty is of no account. But she alone knows how to tend the golden apples that keep the gods young. If we carry her away we shall destroy the apples."

The brothers press forward to seize Freia, but their way is barred by Donner and Froh, who hasten over the hilltop.

"Back, fools!" shouts the thunder god, raising his hammer. The giants lift their clubs in defiance.

Suddenly Wotan stretches his spear between the combatants. "Stop!"

Wotan springs to his feet in anger.

he cries imperiously, as the motive of the *Treaty* thunders in the orchestra:

"I made this pact. Its terms are engraved on the shaft of my spear, and I must defend it or lose my power forever."

The gods are in despair. Who will now save Freia? But, as Wotan turns away, looking anxiously for Loge, a nimble creature clad in fluttering scarlet darts up the mountainside. In a moment the fire god stands before them.

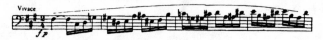

"Where have you been?" asks Wotan. "Come, name Freia's ransom."

"I have searched through all the world," Loge replies; "but nowhere did I find anything more valued by men than the love of women. Only one creature has turned from it. Alberich, the Nibelung, renounced love for the sake of power and robbed the Rhinemaidens of their gold. They cry to you for help, Wotan."

"How can I help them when I am in peril myself," the god replies angrily.

Fasolt and Fafner have listened closely to Loge's tale, and now they ask him what powers the gold possesses that the dwarf should value it so highly. The fire god describes the fearful might of Alberich's Ring. At once all are seized with a desire to own it. The giants declare they are willing to accept the Nibelung's gold in place of Freia, but Wotan wants the Ring himself.

"How can I give you what isn't mine?" he cries. "Shall I steal the dwarf's treasure only to give it to you?"

In answer the giants seize Freia. "We will return tonight," they declare. "But if you don't have the Rhinegold to pay as ransom, the goddess shall be ours forever." Dragging the terrified maiden with them, they stalk through the pass.

A pale mist descends over the mountain, and in its light the gods seem gray and old. Loge peers from one to another in mock anxiety.

"Why, what has happened?" he cries. "Ah, I know! Without Freia the golden apples wither on the bough. You have lost your youth."

Wotan starts up. "Come, Loge!" he cries. "Let us go to Nibelheim. Freia must be ransomed." The fire god slips into a steaming cleft in the rock. As Wotan follows, the mountain is swallowed up in billowing clouds. Dimly a rocky chasm looms in the blackness, rising ever upward; a ruddy glow shines in the distance. Suddenly the clang of anvils is heard on every side:

Then a cavern appears.

Scene Three. Alberich drags Mime from a crevice. "Give me the helmet," he commands, pinching the dwarf savagely.

"Let me alone," screeches Mime. "It is not finished yet."

Alberich leaps at him. In terror the gnome drops a piece of metal-work he has been hiding behind his back, and snatching it up Alberich slips the Tarnhelm on his head. A sinister theme, the *Magic Power of the Helm,* is heard:

In an instant Alberich vanishes. Mime looks about him in astonishment, but the next minute he cowers before the blows of his invisible foe.

As Alberich storms away in triumph, Loge and Wotan climb down through a crevice in the rock. "Who has hurt you, Mime?" asks the fire god, bending over the gnome. Mime tells the strangers how Alberich has enslaved the Nibelungs by the might of the magic Ring, forcing them to dig treasure for him out of the depths of the earth. The motive of *Bondage* wails again and again in the orchestra.

Sobbing, the dwarf describes the powers of the Tarnhelm, which he himself had been obliged to forge and had hoped to keep and use against his brother.

Suddenly a host of gnomes swarms into the cavern. Driven by Alberich, they heap the gold they are carrying into a glittering pile.

"Now back to your anvils and shafts!" shouts the Nibelung harshly. Muttering a charm, he draws the Ring from his finger and, as the theme of *Alberich's Power* rises to a terrifying climax in the orchestra, he stretches it toward his cowering vassals.

With wild shrieks they flee into the crevices.

The presence of the two gods has not escaped the dwarf, and now, turning to them, he asks suspiciously what they want.

"Tales of your mighty power have reached our ears," answers Wotan. "We have come to see these wonders for ourselves."

"Then look there, at the gleaming hoard," their host cries fiercely. "With it I shall conquer Valhalla and force the world to my will. As I renounced love, so all of you shall renounce it!"

Wotan springs to his feet in anger, but quickly Loge steps in front of him. "We are amazed at your power, O dwarf," he says humbly. "But are you not afraid someone might steal the Ring while you are asleep?"

Laughing scornfully, Alberich answers that with the Tarnhelm he can transform himself into any shape he wishes, and so protect himself from harm. To prove his boast he slips on the magic cap. At once he disappears, and in his place a monster snake writhes on the cavern floor. Loge pretends to be terrified.

"What a fearful snake!" he gasps, as the dwarf reappears. "But can you also shrink into something quite small—such as a toad? Surely that would be too difficult, even for you."

Eager to show his skill, Alberich dons his cap and disappears.

The fire god leaps forward. "Quick, seize him!" he shouts, pointing to a tiny toad that crawls at their feet. Wotan pins the creature with his foot, and Loge tears off the Tarnhelm. Then, hastily binding the struggling dwarf, the gods drag him up the shaft by which they came down.

As they vanish into the blackness, the clang of anvils is again heard, the rocky gorge seems to sink, and, climbing up through the cleft in the rock, the travelers arrive on the mountain height with their prisoner.

Scene Four. The Nibelung is furious at having been tricked, and threatens fearful vengeance if he is not released.

"Give me the hoard as ransom and you shall go free," Wotan promises.

Alberich has no choice but to obey. Kissing his Ring, he whispers a secret command, and, as the wailing cry of *Bondage* is heard, the gnomes stagger up with the treasure.

"Pile it there, and be off to your work," orders the fettered lord of Nibelheim, hiding his face in shame from his bondsmen, who scurry back into the earth in terror. Alberich turns to Wotan.

"There is the ransom. Now give me back the Tarnhelm and let me go."

Instead Loge tosses the helmet onto the heap of gold. Wotan gazes at his captive coldly.

"There is a ring on your finger that I desire."

"The Ring!" Alberich turns pale. "Take my life, but not this Ring."

"Do what you wish with your life," the god responds. "The Ring shall be mine!" Seizing Alberich's hand, he wrenches away the Ring. With a fearful cry, the dwarf slumps to the ground. Loge loosens his bonds.

"Slip away home," he taunts. "You are free."

The Nibelung raises himself slowly.

"Free!! Am I really free?" A sinister motive, the *Nibelung's Work of Destruction*, sounds in the orchestra, and Alberich laughs savagely.

Un poco adagio

"Then hear my first greeting to freedom. As the Ring was won by a curse, so I lay *my* curse upon it.

May it bring death to all who possess it, envy and hate to those who do not—till at last it returns to the Nibelung." He rushes to the cleft and vanishes.

The other gods return, followed by the giants and their prisoner. Fasolt is very unwilling to part with Freia.

"If I must take the gold instead," he declares, "heap the ransom so that her lovely form is hidden. As long as I can see her, I will not part with her."

Driving their stakes into the ground before the goddess, the giants pile up the gold. Fafner presses it together greedily. "Here, fill up this hole," he calls. The last of the nuggets is gone, and reluctantly Loge flings on the Tarnhelm. Now at last Freia is ransomed. But wait. Through a tiny hole Fasolt can still see her eyes. The gap must be filled.

"Fools!" cries Loge impatiently. "Can't you see there is no more gold?"

"Then give us the Ring on Wotan's finger," Fafner insists.

The god refuses angrily; what he has won he shall keep for himself. In vain the others implore him to relent. The giants drag Freia roughly from behind the hoard and start toward the pass. Then suddenly the mountaintop is plunged into darkness. A bluish light breaks from a cleft in the earth, and a mysterious form rises slowly from the depths. It is Erda, goddess of eternal wisdom.

"Give up the Ring, Wotan," she warns. "Fly from its terrible curse. A day of disaster is dawning for the gods, so hear me: give up the Ring!" She sinks into the chasm and daylight returns.

Wotan flings the Ring onto the hoard.

At once the giants set about dividing the treasure, each trying to get the larger share. Fasolt snatches the Ring. But as he leaps back, clutching the prize, Fafner strikes out viciously with his staff. Fasolt falls dead. The ominous motive of *Alberich's Curse* rises triumphantly in the orchestra. Horrified, the gods watch in silence as Fafner packs the gold into a huge bag, swings it to his shoulders and shuffles off.

Heavy clouds have gathered. Donner mounts a rock and, swinging his hammer, summons a thunderstorm to clear the air. As he strikes the rock there is a blinding flash, a roar of thunder. Then the mists lift.

On the crag beyond, Valhalla gleams in the light of the setting sun, and a rainbow stretches across the valley to its gates like a mighty bridge. Wotan leads Fricka towards it. But as he reaches the gorge the voices of the Rhinemaidens float up from the river below, pleading for the return of their stolen gold.

"Bid them be silent!" the god shouts angrily, and turns again to the splendid dwelling for which he has paid such an evil price. The plaint of the maidens dies away; as all but Loge cross into Valhalla, the curtain falls slowly.

Die Walküre

PRINCIPAL CHARACTERS *(in order of appearance)*:

Siegmund (tenor), a strange warrior.
Sieglinde (soprano), lovely wife of Hunding.
Hunding (bass), a savage tribal chieftain.
Wotan (bass-baritone), ruler of the gods.
Brünnhilde (soprano), his daughter, a wild Valkyrie maiden.
Fricka (mezzo-soprano), wife of Wotan, and goddess of marriage.

ACT ONE. Years have passed since the gods entered into Valhalla. On earth, a fierce storm is raging in a lonely wood. At last the downpour changes to a gentle patter, and the curtain rises on the interior of Hunding's dwelling. In the center of the dimly lit hall stands a mighty ash tree. its branches thrusting up through the roof above.

Suddenly the door is flung open, and a man enters. Seeing no one, he stretches out wearily on a heap of rugs before the hearth.

A young woman comes in hastily from the inner room. She stops in surprise at seeing a stranger, then bends over him anxiously. "Can he be hurt?" she wonders. The warrior raises his head and begs for a drink of water. His weakness arouses her *Pity:*

Quickly she fetches a draught from the well outside. He gulps it down.

As he lowers the drinking horn their eyes meet, and a lovely melody, the theme of *Love*, sounds softly in the orchestra:

"You have brought me new strength," the young man whispers. "Tell me who you are."

Sieglinde turns away. "This house and I both belong to Hunding. Will you not wait till he returns?" Going to the storeroom, she brings a horn of mead, which she offers to him with friendly eagerness. He empties the horn, and again they gaze into each other's eyes. At last he speaks.

"You have befriended one who is followed everywhere by misfortune," he says sadly. "Rather than risk bringing it to you, I must go." He hastens to the door, but, as he lifts the latch, Sieglinde calls to him wildly to stay.

"You can never bring misfortune where it already dwells," she cries. Mournfully, the motive of the *Wälsung Race* sounds deep in the orchestra:

The stranger returns quietly.

Suddenly the clatter of horse's hoofs rings on the stones outside. Sieglinde hastens to open the door. On the threshold stands the haughty master of the house.

Hunding stares questioningly at the stranger, and Sieglinde explains that she found him lying exhausted on their hearth. Then she sets about preparing supper.

Hunding glances uneasily from the warrior to his wife. "How strangely they resemble one another," he mutters. Hiding his wonder, he offers his guest a place at the table below the ash tree.

"Fight for Hunding!"
cries Wotan. "The Wälsung must fall."

"My name is Hunding," he says. "What is *yours*, and where do you come from?"

"I call myself Woeful," the stranger begins, "for my whole life has been filled with misfortune. Returning from the hunt when I was a youth, my father, Wolf, and I found our home in ruins, my mother slain, and my sister kidnapped. We fled to the woods, and from there waged war with our enemies for years. Then, one day, my father and I were separated in battle. I searched everywhere for him, but all I ever found was an empty wolf skin." The *Valhalla* motive sounds softly, as though to suggest that Wolf may have been a god in disguise.

"It is plain the Fates do not love you," Hunding breaks in roughly "No one wants to have a man like you for a guest."

"Only cowards fear a weaponless stranger," cries Sieglinde, her eyes flashing angrily. She turns to the young man and asks what brought him to their dwelling.

"A young girl, about to be forced into marriage against her will, begged me to help her," he replies. "In the struggle her brothers were killed. Vowing vengeance, her kinsmen rose against me in force. For a long time I defended her against their furious attacks. But, at last the weapons were hewn from my hands, the maiden was slain, and I fled here through the woods." He rises sadly and walks to the hearth as the motive of the *Heroism of the Wälsungs* swells in the orchestra:

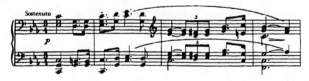

Hunding springs to his feet. "Today I was summoned to avenge the death of a kinsman," he declares grimly. "But I came too late—the murderer had fled. Now I find him in my own home." He advances threateningly. "The laws of hospitality oblige me to shelter you tonight, Wolf's son. But tomorrow you shall pay with your life."

Sieglinde slips between the angry men.

"Leave us!" shouts Hunding furiously. "Go prepare my evening draught."

Sieglinde hastily prepares the drink. Then, turning to the stranger, she tries to direct his attention to a spot on the ash tree. He does not understand, and Hunding drives her before him out of the hall.

The stranger looks after them in despair. He has fallen in love with the wife of his enemy, and longs to save her from her cruel husband. But he is weaponless. Suddenly he remembers that his father had promised him a sword in time of need.

"Wälse! Wälse!" he cries wildly. "Where is your sword?"

As though in answer the fire blazes up and casts its glow across the room. Something gleams brightly in the tree trunk. The warrior looks up eagerly, but the glow fades, and he stretches out to sleep. All is quiet.

Suddenly the inner door opens and Sieglinde steals to his side. "I have drugged my husband," she whispers. "You must flee while he sleeps."

"Not without you," the young man replies ardently.

"Then let me show you a weapon. If you can make it yours, you shall be the mightiest of heroes." Swiftly she tells him the story of her life. Robbers had sold her to Hunding, and, as she sat at her wedding feast, a strange old man entered the hall and plunged a sword into the tree.

All the guests tried to pull it out, but in vain. "Then I knew he put it there for the one who is to save me," cries Sieglinde. "O, when shall I find him? When shall I have vengeance for all I have suffered?"

The warrior sweeps her into his arms. "I shall avenge you," he shouts. With a crash the door at the back swings open and moonlight floods the hall. Drawing Sieglinde down on the couch. the young man tells her that he loves her:

"Spring has come to unite us!" he cries.

"You are the spring that fills my heart," she answers, her face radiant with joy. She gazes at him in wonder. "But surely I have seen you before! Your face and voice are so familiar. And those eyes—gleaming and brave like the eyes of the old man. . . ." She catches her breath in excitement. "Was your father's name really Wolf?"

"He was a wolf to craven foxes," he answers. "His real name was Wälse."

Sieglinde springs wildly to her feet. "Then you are Siegmund, and the sword was struck into the tree for you alone!"

With a bound the hero leaps onto the table and seizes the gleaming hilt. "Yes, I am Siegmund, and this is my rightful sword. As I have found you in my hour of need, so I name you Needful, O sword!" With a mighty wrench he pulls the blade from the tree and shows it to the delighted Sieglinde. "Come, away," he urges. "The spring calls to us. . . ."

She faces him in excitement. "I am Sieglinde," she cries. "You have rescued your own sister."

Siegmund embraces her joyfully. "Long life to the Wälsungs," he shouts, and hand in hand they rush out into the moonlit night.

ACT TWO. As the lovers flee wildly through the forest, their breathless haste is echoed in the orchestra:

Then the hoofbeats of a Valkyrie steed ring out:

The curtain rises on a rocky gorge. Wotan strides up the pass clad in full armor. On a crag above stands Brünnhilde.

"Saddle your horse," Wotan calls to her. "You must shield Siegmund in his coming fight with Hunding."

The Valkyrie answers with a ringing battle cry. "Hojo-to-ho!" she shouts, leaping from rock to rock:

At the peak she stops for a moment.

"Beware, Father," she calls back. "Fricka is coming, and she seems to be very angry." Laughing, the maiden bounds away among the rocks.

Fricka strides haughtily up the ravine and pauses before Wotan. "As goddess of marriage, I have come to ask your help in avenging the wrong done Hunding," she declares. "Siegmund has stolen his wife."

The god points out that Sieglinde was forced into marriage against her will. "She loves Siegmund," he urges. "Let us help them."

"Then the honor of the gods is ended," Fricka bursts out furiously. "Ever since you disguised yourself as Wälse and started the Wälsung race, you have despised us gods."

Wotan explains that he has upheld the Wälsungs only because he needs a free hero to accomplish a deed that will save the gods from destruction.

Fricka laughs scornfully. What could a mortal do that the gods cannot do better? Besides Siegmund is not free. Was it not Wotan who placed the sword in the tree and then led his son to Hunding's hut that he might find it and rescue Sieglinde?

The god turns away angrily, and the motive expressing his *Rage* mutters in the orchestra:

"What do you want of me?" he asks.

"Renounce the Wälsung!"

Gloomily, Wotan agrees not to help Siegmund. But still Fricka is not satisfied. He must order Brünnhilde also to desert the Wälsung.

Fury mounts in Wotan's heart. "I cannot defeat him," he bursts out. "He has found my sword."

"Then destroy its power, let it shatter in his hands." The joyous shout of the Valkyrie rings from the heights above. "There comes your warrior maiden," cries Fricka. "Tell her that today she must fight for *my* honor; she must protect Hunding. Do you promise?"

"Yes, I promise."

Fricka sweeps away in triumph, and the god throws himself down on a rock seat in despair. "I am the most wretched of beings!" he laments.

The Valkyrie descends the crag in alarm. Flinging away her weapons, she rushes to Wotan's side. "Father, what has happened?" she cries.

The god tells her the fateful story of the theft of the gold and of his greed. "Erda warned me of the end of the gods," he says gloomily. "Hoping to find some way of escaping my fate, I visited her in the earth. She bore me nine daughters—you and your sister Valkyries—to help build an army to fight the Nibelung hordes. Fearless and bold, you ride through the sky, bearing heroes who have died in battle to Valhalla to swell our hosts. But this cannot save us. We are all powerless before the might of the Ring.

"Fafner, the giant, has turned himself into a dragon, and guards the hoard in a cavern. But some day he, too, must fall a victim to Alberich's Curse. That is the day I fear. For if Alberich ever recaptures the Ring, the gods are doomed.

"I, myself, cannot wrest the Ring from Fafner," the god goes on, "because I am bound by my Treaty with the giants. Instead I must find a hero who will slay the dragon without my help, and keep the Ring from Alberich. It was for this deed that I created Siegmund, but now Fricka has shown me that he is only a slave."

He starts to his feet in bitter wrath. "Then fade away, glittering splendor. Let all I have built crash in ruins. I only await the end!"

Filled with alarm, Brünnhilde asks how she can help him.

"Fight for Fricka's slave," he answers. "The Wälsung must fall!"

"But you love Siegmund," the Valkyrie cries in despair. "You have taught me to love him. I cannot desert him now."

The god turns on her furiously. "Do you dare defy me?" he shouts. "Beware! My vengeance would crush you. Siegmund falls!" He storms away among the rocks, leaving Brünnhilde to gather up her armor.

"Alas, my Wälsung," she sighs. "I, too, must betray you." She starts down the gorge, but sees the lovers hastening upward and hides in a cave at one side.

Sieglinde staggers up the rocky path, followed by Siegmund. "Don't you hear the horns?" she screams, half mad with fear. "Hunding has awakened from his sleep and called all his savage tribe to the chase. . . ." She stares through the gathering dusk in horror, imagining that she sees the hounds tearing at her lover. "No sword can save you now," she shrieks, and sinks fainting in his arms. Siegmund lays her on the ground and bends over her anxiously.

Night falls. Suddenly the moon rises above the hills. Its clear, cold light falls on Brünnhilde, who approaches silently, like a messenger of *Fate*.

"Siegmund," she calls, "I have come to warn you of your death. You must go with me to Valhalla."

The hero looks up quietly. "Shall Sieglinde come, too?" he asks.

"No. She must remain here on earth."

"Then I shall not go with you," he replies defiantly.

"Death will force you to come," the warrior maiden answers. "He who gave you the sword has taken away its power."

Siegmund bends over Sieglinde in despair. "Must I leave you helpless and alone?" he mourns. "Ah, no! Rather than that I will slay us both."

Deeply moved, Brünnhilde urges him to leave his wife with her. But the Wälsung draws his sword savagely.

"No one shall protect her but me," he shouts, pointing his weapon at Sieglinde's breast. "Here are two lives for you, treacherous steel. Take them with one stroke."

The Valkyrie turns the blow aside with her shield. "You shall both live," she cries impulsively. "I will help you." Bidding him prepare for battle, she rushes away into the darkness.

Suddenly the harsh blare of Hunding's horns sounds through the ravine. Siegmund kisses Sieglinde tenderly. Then, sword in hand, he plunges into the black clouds that have swept up, covering the mountainside. Left alone, Sieglinde stirs uneasily in her sleep. There is a crash of thunder, and she springs to her feet in terror.

"Siegmund!" she screams. "Where are you?"

The clouds part and she sees him on the crag above in furious combat with Hunding. Brünnhilde stands by the hero, sheltering him with her shield. But, as he leans forward to deal the fatal blow, a red glare breaks through the clouds and Wotan appears. "Back from the spear!" he roars, thrusting it between the fighters. Siegmund's sword shatters

on the mighty shaft, and Hunding plunges his lance through the
Wälsung's defenseless breast.

Snatching up the broken sword, Brünnhilde flees with Sieglinde.
Wotan strikes Hunding dead with a look of contempt. Then he remembers the Valkyrie's disobedience.

"Woe to you, Brünnhilde!" he shouts, in terrible wrath. "You shall
pay dearly." Amid lightning and thunder he storms off in pursuit.

ACT THREE. The wild gallop of Valkyrie steeds sounds as the warrior
maidens ride through the sky, bearing heroes to Valhalla. Then the
curtain rises on a mountaintop. Four Valkyries in full armor stand on
a jagged peak, gazing off into the storm-filled sky. "Hojo-to-ho!" they
shout. Dark clouds roll past, and answering shouts echo up from below.
The other Valkyries swarm up the rock. "Where is Brünnhilde?"
they cry.

"There she comes, urging her horse to reckless speed," calls one.

"Why, she has a woman with her!" exclaims another.

Brünnhilde hastens in with Sieglinde. "Help me, sisters," she gasps.
"Wotan is pursuing me." The Valkyries start back in dismay. From the
north a terrible blackness is sweeping down on the rock, and the fierce
neighing of Wotan's horse sounds in the shriek of the wind. "Lend me
a fresh steed," Brünnhilde implores. "If Wotan finds Sieglinde here he
will destroy her." But she pleads in vain. The frightened Valkyries dare
not defy the god, and in despair Brünnhilde turns to Sieglinde. The
maiden repulses her coldly.

"Why didn't you let me die with Siegmund?" she mourns. "Ah, if
you really want to help me, plunge your sword into my heart."

"You must live," Brünnhilde exclaims, "for you are to be the mother
of Siegmund's child."

Radiant with sudden joy, Sieglinde flings herself at Brünnhilde's feet
and implores her help.

"Then flee alone," the Valkyrie answers. "I will stay here and wait
for Wotan." She tells Sieglinde to hide in the forest where Fafner
guards the Nibelung Hoard, as Wotan avoids the place.

"Be brave, for your son, Siegfried, shall be the world's most glorious
hero," she says.

"Some day he will forge these fragments of his father's sword and do mighty deeds."

"You have given me hope." Sieglinde cries gratefully, taking the splintered sword, and the motive of the *Power of Love* soars upward:

"Perhaps Sieglinde's blessing will bring you joy in the future." She hastens away as black clouds surround the peak.

"Stay, Brünnhilde," roars the angry god. Terrified, the Valkyrie shrinks behind her sisters. Wotan strides up the slope. "Where is Brünnhilde?" he rages. "Where is the traitoress who hides, like a coward, from the doom she has earned?"

Brünnhilde comes forward quietly. "Here I am, Father. Tell me what my fate is to be."

"You have shaped it yourself," he answers violently. "I made you a Valkyrie to carry out my wishes, but you choose to carry out your own instead. You have lost the right to be a goddess. Bound in sleep, you shall be left on this rock for the first man who comes along to awaken and claim as his own."

Brünnhilde sinks to the ground in despair. Horror-struck, the Valkyries beg Wotan to relent. He turns on them furiously.

"Does her fate frighten you? Then begone, or you shall share it!" With wild cries the maidens scatter in flight, leaving Brünnhilde at Wotan's feet. The storm clouds sweep away and sunset gleams on the distant horizon.

At last Brünnhilde raises herself. "Was my deed really so shameful that I should be robbed of honor forever?" she asks softly. "I knew that you loved the Wälsung and that Fricka forced you to forsake him against your will."

"You knew that, and yet disobeyed me?"

Brünnhilde tells Wotan of her meeting with Siegmund. "I saw the hero's bitter sorrow," she cries, "and my heart commanded me to help him." She gazes tenderly at Wotan. "It was you who first placed me at Siegmund's side. In helping him, I was true to your secret wishes."

"You did what I would so gladly have done myself," the god replies bitterly. "Now you must pay the penalty of your disobedience."

"Then let the man who wakens me be worthy," Brünnhilde pleads, and tells him that Sieglinde has saved the greatest of the Wälsung heroes. But the god refuses to hear about the ill-fated race. He cannot change her punishment.

In despair Brünnhilde throws herself at his feet. "Kill me," she implores wildly, "but don't let me fall into the hands of a coward." Suddenly she leaps to her feet, her eyes flashing with excitement. "Command a fire to surround me. Let it drive back all but the bravest!"

At last Wotan's anger is gone and he sweeps her into his arms. "Farewell, my glorious child," he cries. "We must part forever. But I will kindle a fire for you that all the world shall fear. Only one—the mightiest of heroes—shall pass through and waken you. Now farewell!"

He kisses her tenderly, and the mysterious chords of *Eternal Sleep* steal downward:

Brünnhilde sinks unconscious in his arms:

The god carries her to a rocky mound under a pine tree and covers her with her shield. Mounting the crag, he strikes it with his spear.

"Hither, Loge," he shouts. A flash of flame leaps up. Wotan directs it with his spear; it darts flickering from rock to rock, until at last the whole mountaintop is surrounded by a wall of fire. "Only he who does not fear my spear shall conquer the flames," cries the god.

Below him, the firelight glints on the armor of the sleeping Valkyrie, and for a moment he gazes down sadly. Then, turning, he plunges through the flames and vanishes into the night.

Siegfried

PRINCIPAL CHARACTERS *(in order of appearance):*

Mime (tenor), the cringing, cowardly brother of Alberich. After the gods stole the Nibelung Ring?, the dwarf left Nibelheim and set up his forge in a cave, deep in the gloomy forest where Fafner guards the Hoard.

Siegfried (tenor), a wild youth, whom Mime has raised as his son.

The Wanderer (bass-baritone), a strange old man.

Alberich (baritone), the evil Nibelung who stole the Rhinegold.

Fafner (bass), the giant, transformed by the Tarnhelm into a dragon.

Voice of the Forest Bird (soprano).

Erda (contralto), mysterious goddess of wisdom.

Brünnhilde (soprano), the wild Valkyrie maiden, whom Wotan bound in magic slumber and left on a crag surrounded by fire.

THE PRELUDE begins ominously. Over and over again the clanging motive of the *Forge* is heard, followed by the wail of *Bondage*. Then a menacing theme sounds deep in the orchestra:

In *Rheingold* it described the *Gathering of the Hoard* by the Nibelung dwarfs; now Fafner guards the glittering treasure that all the world longs to possess, and, surging upward, the music thunders to a fearful climax. The theme of the *Ring* sounds fatefully. Then, in a sudden silence, the motive of Siegmund's *Sword* rings out like a promise of heroic deeds to come. As the clang of the forge returns, the curtain rises on the dim interior of a large cave.

ACT ONE. Mime is hunched over the anvil, hammering away at a sword. "Senseless work!" he mutters angrily. "The weapons I make are strong enough for a giant, but Siegfried snaps them into bits." He throws aside the blade. "The boy wouldn't be able to break Needful," he reflects. "If only I could mend the mighty fragments, he would slay Fafner for me, and the gold would be mine. . . ." He tears his matted locks in despair. "But I can't forge Needful."

A merry horn call sounds in the woods:

A minute later a tall youth bursts into the cave, driving a bear before him.

"Ask for the sword, Bruin," he shouts. The dwarf scuttles behind the forge in fear.

"There it is," he shrieks.

Laughing, Siegfried sends the bear away and takes up the weapon.

"Why, what kind of toy is this?" he exclaims angrily, snapping the blade in his powerful hands. "I wish I had broken it on your head." Raging, he throws himself on a pile of rugs at one side.

Mime approaches him cautiously. "What ingratitude!" he whines. "This is my reward for teaching the nasty little brat all I know."

Siegfried turns and looks at him. "You have taught me many things, Mime, but not how to stand the sight of you. If you are so clever, tell me what it is that makes me return to the cave."

"Young ones always come back to the nest," the smith answers. "You love Mimi just as the little birds love their father."

"The animals taught me what love is, not you," Siegfried declares indignantly.

"But I have noticed that there is always a mother as well as a father. Where is your wife, Mime? Did you make me all by yourself?"

Angrily the dwarf tells him that he is both father and mother.

"You lie!" shouts Siegfried. "Children are like their parents. I saw myself in the brook, and I am as different from you as a toad is from a gleaming fish. Now I know why I come back—it is to find out who were my father and mother."

"You have no other parents," the dwarf mutters hastily, but Siegfried seizes him by the throat. Shrieking, Mime agrees to tell all he knows. The motives of the *Wälsung Race* and *Pity* sound softly.

"Once I found a woman lying exhausted in the woods," the dwarf begins, and tells how he helped Sieglinde to the cave, where she died when the boy was born.

"If you expect me to believe your story, show me some proof," Siegfried insists. Mime thinks a moment. Then he takes Siegmund's broken sword from its hiding place and shows it to the boy.

"Your mother told me it was shattered when your father was killed."

"Then this is the right sword for me!" exults Siegfried. "Hurry and forge it, for today I shall leave you forever and seek my fortune in the world."

Before Mime can stop him he rushes off into the woods.

The dwarf is in despair. "Now how can I get him to kill Fafner?" he moans. "My skill will never mend this stubborn sword."

Suddenly a voice hails him from the shadows in the rear of the cave. "Greetings, smith! A weary traveler would like to rest by your hearth."

Mime starts up fearfully. "Who is there?" he quavers, looking around.

An old man dressed in a long cloak and carrying a mighty spear comes slowly forward.

"I am known as the Wanderer," he says.

"In my travels I have learned much. Perhaps I can help you."

"I know enough for my needs," snaps Mime. "Be off!"

Instead, the Wanderer seats himself by the forge. "I stake my head in a battle of wits," he declares. "Ask me three questions."

The dwarf ponders how he may rid himself of his guest. "Tell me what races live in the earth—on its surface—and in the sky," he asks.

"The Nibelungs dwell in the earth," the Wanderer replies. "The giants live on its broad surface, and the gods in the clouds above. Wotan. their leader. rules all the world by the power of his mighty spear." As he speaks, the Wanderer touches his spear to the ground. There is a clap of thunder, a flash of light. Mime cringes in terror, for he recognizes the stranger as none other than Wotan himself.

"You have saved your head," he stammers, trembling, "now go on your way."

But the Wanderer replies that by the laws of compact Mime. too, must answer three questions. "Tell me, honorable dwarf," he begins, "what is the race that Wotan loves, yet treats with great harshness?"

"The Wälsungs," cries Mime, recovering from his fright.

"And with what sword will Siegfried kill Fafner?"

The dwarf rubs his hands gleefully. "With Needful," he declares.

"Good," laughs the Wanderer. "But there is yet another question. Who will forge Needful's mighty. splinters?"

Mime starts to his feet. "I don't know who will mend the blade," he screams, throwing his tools about in despair.

Wotan rises quietly. "When you had the opportunity, you should have asked what you really needed to know. Now the wager is lost. 'Only he who knows no fear shall forge Needful,' and I leave your head forfeit to him." As he departs, flickering light fills the cave. Mime imagines he hears the dragon crashing through the woods to eat him, and shrinks in terror behind the anvil.

Siegfried bounds through the doorway. "Why, what were you doing down there?" he asks, laughing, as Mime crawls from his hiding place. "Is the sword ready yet?"

The dwarf thinks quickly. His head is forfeit to him who knows no fear, and Siegfried is not afraid of anything. He must teach the boy to fear, or he will be lost. "I have been thinking about you," he tells Siegfried. "Your mother warned me not to let you go away before you had learned to fear."

"Who will teach me?" the youth asks eagerly.

"A monster dragon lives at the far end of the wood," Mime responds. "He will teach you fear."

"Good!" exclaims Siegfried. "But now forge me the sword."

Mime tells him that only he who knows no fear can mend Needful.

"Then *I* will forge it," declares the boy. Striding to the hearth, he sets about melting the fragments.

"Needful! Needful!" he sings joyously, as the flames leap up. "Who shattered your mighty steel?"

The dwarf watches anxiously. "He will forge the sword and slay Fafner," he mutters. "But I will brew a poisonous drink to give him when he is thirsty. Then I can cut off his head and win the Ring." Shrieking with delight, he dances about the cave. "Alberich will be my bondsman," he gloats. "Hei, Mime, prince of the gnomes, now you will rule the world."

Siegfried hammers the hot steel into shape on the anvil. "Awake to new life, Needful!" he shouts, swinging the finished sword. "Look, Mime. See how Siegfried's sword cuts!" With a mighty blow he slashes the anvil in two.

ACT TWO. A dark, gloomy prelude describes the depths of the forest where Fafner guards the Hoard. Alberich's *Curse* sounds savagely, as though warning of the fate of all who possess the Ring. Then the motive of the *Nibelung's Work of Destruction* mutters deep in the orchestra, and the curtain rises on a forest glade before the dragon's den.

There, among the gnarled tree trunks that thrust up into the black night, lurks Alberich, waiting for a chance to seize the Ring again. Sudden gusts of wind sweep through the underbrush, as though someone were coming. Then the clouds part, and moonlight falls on the Wanderer, standing before the cave.

Alberich starts back. "What are you doing here, thief?" he screams furiously. "Begone, for you are bound by your Treaty with the giants and cannot snatch the Ring."

"Don't quarrel with me," answers the Wanderer. "Quarrel with Mime. He is bringing a hero to slay the dragon and win him the gold. Why don't you warn Fafner? Perhaps he will give you the Ring." Going toward the cavern, Wotan calls to the monster to awaken.

"A hero is coming to kill you, worm," shouts Alberich. "Let me have the Ring and you will be safe."

The dragon's voice rumbles up from the black depths of the cave. "I will keep what I have," he growls. "Let me sleep."

Laughing, the Wanderer advises Alberich to be on his guard against Mime, and storms off. The dwarf looks after him angrily.

"Scoff away," he mutters. "But so long as the gold is in the world, my curse shall work for your downfall." He slips into a crevice as the pale light of dawn penetrates the tangled branches.

Mime and Siegfried come through the forest. "This is the place," whispers the dwarf, fearfully. "Soon you will see the dragon, and your heart will pound with fright."

Driving Mime away, Siegfried stretches out on a mossy bank and gazes up at the treetops. Sunlight gleams on the fluttering leaves, and all about him the forest murmurs softly. "How glad I am that Mime is no kin of mine," the boy muses. "Surely my father must have looked like me. But what was my mother like? And why did she die and leave me alone?"

Above him, a woodbird twitters joyfully:

Siegfried listens with growing interest; then, jumping up, he cuts a reed pipe and tries to imitate the warbler. But his pipe squeaks harshly. "I guess I'm too dull to speak your language. little bird," the boy chuckles. "Listen instead to a tune on my horn. How often have I played it, hoping to find a comrade. Let us see who will come today." He sets the horn to his lips and blows lustily.

As the notes ring through the forest there is a sudden stir in the cave. A monster dragon lifts its head and glares at the boy with cruel eyes. "I came out to drink," it roars. "Now I find food as well."

Siegfried laughs merrily. "What a lovely playmate! Watch out, growler, my sword has a keen edge."

Breathing out clouds of fiery smoke, Fafner crawls down the slope. But the boy leaps forward fearlessly; as the monster rears to crush him, he plunges Needful into its savage heart. The dragon falls with a crash.

"Beware, valiant youth!" gasps the dying beast. "The Ring with its terrible curse has brought about my death; it will bring about yours also." With a last moan, Fafner rolls over dead.

Siegfried draws out his sword. The dragon's blood burns his finger and quickly he puts it in his mouth. Suddenly he understands the birds.

"Hei, Siegfried," calls the warbler who sang to him before. "If you take the Ring and Tarnhelm from the treasure you will become lord of the world."

As Siegfried goes into the cave, Mime and Alberich slink from opposite sides of the glade. each intent on snatching the Ring. "Where are you sneaking, rogue?" snarls Alberich. "Are you after my gold?"

"It's mine, not yours," shrieks Mime defiantly. "I raised the boy for this deed. and I won't be robbed of my wage."

Siegfried appears in the mouth of the cave, and hastily the dwarfs scuttle back to their hiding places. Again the bird advises the boy. "You have won the Ring," she calls. "Now, beware of Mime."

Siegfried turns and sees the dwarf approaching. "Welcome, my hero," whines the gnome. "You must be tired from your fight. But I have a nice drink for you here. Take only a sip. and you'll rest forever."

"So you plan to murder me in my sleep?" cries the boy indignantly.

"What! Did I say that?" asks Mime in vexation, not realizing that, since Siegfried has tasted the dragon's blood. he can read his thoughts.

Overcome with loathing, the boy slays Mime and throws his body inside the cave. "Lie there," he cries harshly. "You wanted the gold; now I give it to you." Then, to protect the treasure from thieves, he shoves the huge frame of the dragon across the entrance. At last the work is done.

Hot and tired, Siegfried throws himself under the linden tree and gazes up at the bird. "I am so lonely," he cries. "Won't you help me find a comrade?"

"A glorious bride lies asleep on a faraway crag," answers the bird. "She is surrounded by fire, and only he who knows no fear may win Brünnhilde."

Siegfried springs up in wild joy. "I am the stupid lad that never learned fear," he shouts. "Lead on, my songster; I will follow you." The bird darts away swiftly, and Siegfried plunges after it, bound for Brünnhilde's rock.

ACT THREE. A violent tempest is raging. The themes of the *Rhine* and of *Erda* sweep stormily upward, accompanied by the galloping rhythm of the Valkyries' *Ride*. Wotan is again seeking the goddess of wisdom. Suddenly, a great downward surge hints that the *Fall of the Gods* is at hand:

The curtain rises on a wild gorge at the foot of a rocky mountain. Striding from among the boulders, the Wanderer stops before a cavern.

"Awaken, Erda!" he shouts. "Arise from the depths."

The mysterious chords of *Eternal Sleep* sound softly, and the goddess rises from the earth. "Who calls me from my sleep?" she demands.

"I summoned you," cries the Wanderer. Hiding his identity, he questions her about the future.

"Once I gave Wotan a wise and courageous daughter." Erda replies. "Why don't you ask her advice?"

"Do you mean Brünnhilde?" cries the stranger violently. "She defied Wotan and now lies bound in magic slumber. How could she help me?"

Erda moves uneasily. "Why should the Valkyrie be punished for carrying out what Wotan planned and what was his dearest wish?" she mourns. "Alas! the world is ruled by falsehood and treachery." Her voice sinks to a whisper. "Let me go! I long to sleep again."

"You shall not go," shouts the Wanderer, and suddenly Erda recognizes the ruler of the gods. "Your wisdom is fading," the Wanderer cries harshly. "You, too, shall perish with the gods. But now, at last, I am content with my fate, for Siegfried shall inherit my power and become master of the earth.

Without my help he has won the Nibelung Ring, and even now approaches to awaken Brünnhilde." He lifts his spear in command. "Away, then, Erda! Descend to eternal sleep." The goddess sinks slowly into the ground. Slipping into the shadows, Wotan awaits Siegfried.

Suddenly the woodbird flutters overhead. It darts away in fear, and a minute later Siegfried clambers up the gorge. "Where are you going, lad?" calls the Wanderer. Siegfried turns in surprise.

"I am seeking a mountain surrounded by fire," he replies. "A maiden is sleeping inside the flaming circle, and I mean to waken her."

The Wanderer is delighted with the boy's courage, and questions him about the sword he is carrying. At last Siegfried grows impatient.

"I have no time for idle chatter, old man," he cries angrily. "Be quick! Either show me the path, or get out of my way."

The motive of Wotan's *Rage* mutters in the orchestra. "I am the guardian of Brünnhilde's rock," the god replies. "He who goes through the fire breaks my power forever. You shall not pass!"

Siegfried laughs. "Go back, boaster, or I will sweep you aside."

Furious, the god bars the way with his spear. "I still hold the shaft that shattered Needful long ago," he roars. "Today it shall smash the blade again."

"Then you are my father's foe," shouts Siegfried. "At last I shall avenge his death." With a furious stroke he slashes the Wanderer's spear in two. There is a crash of thunder, a terrifying flash—then silence.

Wotan stoops and picks up the fragments of his spear. "Go on," he mutters, "I cannot stop you."

He disappears in the shadows. Turning, Siegfried gazes up at the mountain, which is now surrounded by leaping flames. "That is the way to Brünnhilde," he cries joyously, and, sounding his horn, he plunges into the fire. At once the flames rush down and fill the gorge —everything vanishes in the surging, fiery flood.

Then, little by little the flames die down and the Valkyrie rock appears above the glowing mist. Siegfried has climbed the precipice at the back and stands on the summit, staring in wonder at the scene before him. Suddenly the gleam of metal catches his eye. Stretched under a pine in the hollow below lies a figure in shining armor. The boy hastens down the rocky slope and lifts the heavy shield. Then, severing the fastening of the breastplate with his sword, he tosses it aside. Before him lies a sleeping Valkyrie—the first woman he has ever seen.

He starts back in panic—at last he has learned how to fear! Wildly he calls to the maiden to waken, but she does not answer; and in despair he flings himself down and kisses her red lips.

Brünnhilde opens her eyes. She rises slowly, and, as Siegfried watches in wonder, she stretches out her arms in joyous *Greeting to the World:*

"Who is the hero that woke me?" she asks.

"I woke you," answers the youth. "Siegfried is my name."

Wotan's promise is fulfilled, and rapturously Brünnhilde greets the young Wälsung:

But soon her joy turns to sadness. She sees her horse, Grane, grazing on the slope, and realizes that she is no longer a goddess.

Siegfried's ardor frightens her. "In Valhalla all the heroes respected me," she cries, fleeing from his embraces. "Ah, leave me in *Peace.*"

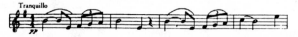

But he cannot leave her. "I love you, Brünnhilde!" he cries. "Be mine."

"I have always been yours," Brünnhilde answers. Casting aside all doubts, she flings herself into his arms at last.

"Now my courage comes back to me!" shouts the hero.

The maiden laughs in wild joy. "Farewell, Valhalla!" she exults. "Farewell, eternal gods! My destiny is with Siegfried."

"We shall live and die together," he answers passionately, and, drawing her close, he kisses her as the curtain falls on the sunlit heights.

Götterdämmerung

(THE TWILIGHT OF THE GODS)

PROLOGUE. The gleaming chords of Brünnhilde's *Greeting to the World* ring out, followed by the murmur of the *Rhine*. Then *Fate* mutters darkly, and the curtain rises on the Valkyrie rock. It is night. The glow of smoldering flames shines through the gloom and lights up three mysterious women who sit beneath the pine tree. A magical rope is in their hands; fastening one end to the tree, they toss the other to and fro among them, weaving the destiny of the world. As they spin, they sing about the terrible events that have happened since the gold was stolen from the Rhine. But Alberich's Curse has weakened the strands of their rope, and suddenly it breaks! Wildly the sisters bind themselves together and sink into the earth.

Then slowly the firelight fades. Sunrise gleams on the horizon. Siegfried's horn call sounds, but in a new, heroic way, as though proclaiming that the carefree boy who killed the dragon has now grown into a man. After it comes the theme of *Brünnhilde:*

As daylight floods the mountaintop, she comes from the cave at one side, followed by Siegfried, who is clad in glittering armor and bears the shield of the Valkyrie.

"Go forth to new deeds, my hero," cries the maiden. "I would not truly love you if I kept you here with me. But never forget the bride for whom you defied the fire, or the oaths we have sworn."

"I shall never forget you," Siegfried replies ardently. "And as proof of my devotion, I give you the Nibelung Ring." In return, Brünnhilde gives him her horse, Grane.

"Now I shall triumph through you alone," Siegfried exults. "Your horse shall carry me and your shield protect me."

Brünnhilde calls on the gods to look down on her happiness. Then, flinging herself into Siegfried's arms, she bids him a last farewell. The hero leads the horse down the mountainside, and Brünnhilde hastens to the summit of the rock, watching for him to reappear in the valley below. At last the notes of his horn echo up. Brünnhilde waves in delight, and, as the curtain falls, the orchestra describes Siegfried's journey down the Rhine. His horn call sounds out merrily, but then the *Rhine* motive surges up, sweeeping everything before it. Suddenly it is interrupted by the theme foretelling the *Fall of the Gods.* The Rhinemaidens' lament rings out, followed by the gleaming notes of the *Gold* motive, and gradually the music becomes dark and threatening. *Alberich's Power* mutters grimly, as though hinting of treachery to come.

ACT ONE. On the banks of the Rhine stands the hall of the Gibichungs, a tribe of savage, Nordic hunters.

Gunther, their weak and hesitating chieftain, sits at the council table with his fair young sister, Gutrune. and his half-brother, Hagen, whose sallow skin and coarse black hair suggest that strange blood flows in his veins.

"Tell me. Hagen." blusters the king, "is my fame along the Rhine worthy of our name?"

"No," retorts Hagen, "for you have no wife, and Gutrune is without a husband." Drawing closer to the others, he tells them he knows of a bride fit for the king. "She is the noblest woman in the world," he whispers, "but her home is surrounded by fire, and only he who defies the flames may win her."

"Can I pass the fire?" asks Gunther anxiously.

"No. Only Siegfried, the dragon-slayer, is able to do that."

The king rises angrily. "Why do you stir me up to want something I can never have?" he bursts out. "How could I force Siegfried to win her for me?"

Hagen stops him with a gesture. "If Gutrune were his wife, he would be glad to serve you," he declares.

"Now you are mocking me, Hagen," protests Gutrune. "Surely Siegfried must have claimed Brünnhilde for himself long ago."

Hagen leans across the table, a strange glitter in his sinister eyes. "Have you forgotten the potion that is hidden in the chest?" he asks. "Some day Siegfried will come to Gibich's land. Then let him taste but one drop of the drink, and he will forget that he ever saw a woman before you." A mysterious theme, suggesting *Magic,* sounds:

At that moment a horn is heard on the Rhine. Hagen looks out. "It is Siegfried," he shouts, and, calling through his cupped hands, he welcomes the hero to their shores. Siegfried drives his boat to land. As he springs ashore, the motive of *Alberich's Curse* thunders ominously.

"Where is the king of the Gibichungs?" he demands. "Let him fight with me or be my friend."

Hastily Gunther offers his friendship. At a sign from Hagen, Gutrune brings Siegfried a long curved drinking horn. "Welcome, guest," she says.

"Gunther's sister begs you to accept this draught."

With a friendly bow, Siegfried takes the horn. "Whatever happens, I shall never forget you, Brünnhilde," he whispers. "I drink this to our love." As he quaffs the fatal draught, the sinister notes of *Magic* mutter in the orchestra. Hagen draws closer, watching the hero with fierce attention. Will the potion work?

Suddenly, Siegfried turns passionately to Gutrune. She leaves the hall in confusion, and he stares after her, bewitched. At last he turns to Gunther.

"How can I win your sister?" he asks.

"I will give you Gutrune if you will help me win the bride I desire," replies the king. "Her home is on a crag surrounded by fire. . . ."

"By fire!" Siegfried exclaims, as though trying to remember something.

"Yes. But I may not pass through. Brünnhilde is beyond my reach."

Even the name of his former bride does not stir Siegfried's clouded memory. "I am not afraid of the fire, and will fetch her for you," he cries. "The Tarnhelm will disguise me so that she will think I am you."

"Then let us swear the oath of blood-brotherhood," says Gunther.

Hagen fills a drinking horn and holds it out to the other two, who scratch their arms with their swords and squeeze a few drops of blood into the horn. "If either of us is false to the friendship pledged today, let him pay with his life," they declare solemnly, and drink.

Then, taking up their weapons, they set out down the Rhine in Siegfried's boat, leaving Hagen to guard the hall.

Arming himself with a massive shield and spear, Hagen takes his place in the doorway. "Siegfried brings Brünnhilde to the Rhine," he gloats. "And with her he brings me the Ring! Sail on, light-hearted hero! Though you scorn him, all of you serve the *Nibelung's son!*"

The curtain falls, and again the orchestra describes Siegfried's trip on the Rhine. But now the *Ring* motive sounds gloomily, and the theme of *Siegfried* rings out, broken and distorted, as though disaster were threatening. Then the theme of *Brünnhilde* sounds, and the curtain rises on the Valkyrie rock.

Brünnhilde sits before the cave, looking at her Ring. Suddenly, thunder rumbles in the distance. The voice of Waltraute, one of the Valkyries, calls from a storm cloud sweeping down over the wood, and Brünnhilde runs to meet her sister.

"Has Wotan pardoned me?" she asks.

"No. In coming here I have broken his command," cries Waltraute wildly. "But a more fearful fate than his vengeance threatens us all. While he was roaming the world as the Wanderer, Wotan's mighty spear was shattered by Siegfried. Now the gods and heroes are gathered in the great hall of Valhalla awaiting their end. Only you can save us." Throwing away her weapons, the Valkyrie flings herself on her knees before Brünnhilde. "Give back the Ring to the Rhinemaidens," she implores. "Rescue us from Alberich's terrible curse!"

"Give back the Ring?" exclaims Brünnhilde. "Siegfried gave it to me as a pledge of his love, and I shall never part with it, even though Valhalla fall in ruins."

Waltraute rushes away in despair. As Brünnhilde looks after her, the fire about the mountain leaps up in flaming fury. Siegfried's horn call rings out, and with a cry of joy Brünnhilde rushes toward the summit to meet him.

A strange warrior leaps through the flame.

"Who are you?" gasps Brünnhilde in horror.

"My name is Gunther," replies the stranger, whose face is hidden by a mesh helmet. "I have come to claim you as my bride." He leaps down.

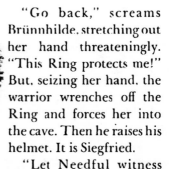

"Go back," screams Brünnhilde, stretching out her hand threateningly. "This Ring protects me!" But, seizing her hand, the warrior wrenches off the Ring and forces her into the cave. Then he raises his helmet. It is Siegfried.

"Let Needful witness that I am true to Gunther," he cries, drawing his sword. Lowering the Tarnhelm again, he follows Brünnhilde.

ACT TWO. It is night. Hagen sits on the outer step of the hall of the Gibichungs, sound asleep. Suddenly, the moon breaks through the clouds and lights up the dark figure of Alberich, who crouches before him.

"Hagen, my son," whispers the Nibelung, "we must gain the Ring at once. For, should Siegfried return it to the Rhine, the gold would be lost forever."

"Have no fear!" mutters Hagen. "*I* shall win the Ring!"

Alberich vanishes, and gradually morning dawns over the Rhine. Siegfried appears on the shore, swinging the Tarnhelm in his hand, and hails Hagen, who wakes with a start. "See how quickly the magic helm brought me here," cries the hero gaily. "Gunther and Brünnhilde are following by boat."

Hagen calls Gutrune out to greet her lover, and Siegfried tells them how he won Gunther's bride for him. "We must give her a worthy greeting," declares Gutrune. "You call the men, Hagen. I will prepare the wedding feast." She goes into the house with Siegfried. Climbing the lookout rock by the river, Hagen blows a loud, harsh blast on his horn.

"Hoi-ho!" he shouts. "Hither, vassals! Come armed for battle, for Gunther is bringing a bride home."

From every side armed men come plunging through the woods. "Where is the enemy?" they shout. "What are your commands, Hagen?"

"Fill the drinking horn and toast the wedding couples," he calls down, but, as the vassals burst into laughter, Hagen cautions them to be faithful to their new mistress and avenge any wrongs she may have suffered.

At last the king's boat rounds the bend. "Hail, Gunther!" shout the men, crowding down to the shore. "Hail to you and your bride."

Gunther acknowledges their greeting proudly, and leads Brünnhilde onto land. But his bride stares gloomily at the ground, and does not even look up when Gutrune and Siegfried come out to welcome them.

"I greet you, sister," cries Gunther. "Two couples are united here today: Brünnhilde and Gunther—Gutrune and Siegfried."

With a start, Brünnhilde raises her eyes. Before her stands Siegfried at the side of a strange woman, and for a moment she sways as if about to faint. Siegfried springs forward to catch her. On his finger gleams the Nibelung Ring.

Brünnhilde starts back in excitement. "That is the Ring you stole from me on the mountaintop, Gunther. How did *he* get it?"

The king cannot answer.

"Then it was Siegfried who broke through the flames and tore the Ring from me," Brünnhilde bursts out furiously. "Ah, gods above, lend me such *Vengeance* as was never seen before!"

She turns to the vassals. "Hear me, all of you! Not Gunther, but Siegfried won me for his wife."

The Gibichungs surge forward in anger. Pushing through the mob, Siegfried calls for a weapon on which to swear to his loyalty. "Swear on my spear," cries Hagen.

At once the vassals form a circle about the two men. Siegfried lays his hand on the weapon.

"Shining steel," he cries, "hear my oath! Brünnhilde's tale is false.

If I have deceived my brother, may your point punish me with death."

Brünnhilde strides angrily into the circle and tears Siegfried's hand from the spear. "Shining steel!" she cries. "Let your vengeance be sure. For the traitor has sworn falsehood on your sacred point."

In wild confusion, all call on the thunder god to avenge this disgrace. Paying no heed to the uproar, Siegfried calls to the men to follow him in to the wedding feast, and soon the shore is deserted. Only Hagen and Gunther remain with the despairing Brünnhilde.

The motive of *Murder* sounds in the orchestra:

"Who will lend me a sword to avenge my shame?" she cries wildly.

Hagen has approached silently from behind. "I will strike down the traitor," he mutters. "His oath was sworn on my spear."

Brünnhilde laughs bitterly. "You! One glance from the hero would destroy you. But wait! There *is* a way to kill him. Strike at his back and he will fall."

Hagen turns to Gunther, who sits at one side, sunk in dejection. "Up, noble Gibichung," he cries harshly. "Siegfried has betrayed you and must pay with his life."

"With his life!" gasps the cowardly monarch in horror.

"Yes. But his downfall will be your gain." Lowering his voice, Hagen reminds his half-brother that the Ring will be his when Siegfried is dead. Still Gunther hesitates. "How could we face Gutrune if we murdered her husband?" he protests.

"She will never know," replies Hagen. "Tomorrow we will go hunting, and we will tell her he was killed by a wild boar." The king agrees to the plot, and all three join in an oath of vengeance. "Soon the Ring will be mine," mutters Hagen triumphantly.

At that moment the wedding procession bursts from the hall. Brünnhilde steps back impetuously, but Hagen forces her to join the revelers with Gunther. As the curtain falls, the theme of *Vengeance* thunders forth.

ACT THREE, *Scene One.* The horns of the hunters ring through the forest. Then the murmur of the *Rhine* is heard, and the curtain rises on a wooded glen that slopes down to the river's edge. It is late afternoon, and the fading sunlight glistens on the waves. The three Rhinemaidens are circling about near the shore.

"O Rhinegold," they lament, "how brightly you once shone!"

Siegfried's horn sounds near by, and the maidens dive below. The hero comes out on a rock overhanging the Rhine. At once the mermaids rise to the surface.

"Siegfried," they call gaily, "We will tell you where your game has hidden if you will give us your Ring."

Laughing, the hero tells them that he killed a dragon for the gold. Shall he give it up for a bearskin? The maidens accuse him of being a miser, and, stung by their taunts, he draws off the Ring to give to them. But now the maidens are serious. "You will gladly give it to us when we tell you of the curse that haunts it," they explain. "Just as you killed Fafner, so you too will be slain today unless you return the gold to the Rhine."

Their warning angers Siegfried. "I would have given you the Ring for love," he says. "But now that you threaten me, you shall not have it."

The maidens swim around wildly. "Come, sisters," they cry. "Leave the madman to his fate." As they disappear, Hagen's horn sounds on the heights above, and the hunting party descends into the glen. The men stretch out to rest. "Is it true," Hagen asks Siegfried, as the drinking horns are being passed around, "that you can understand the speech of the birds?"

"Since women have sung to me, I have forgotten all about them," laughs the hero. His companions urge him to tell of his adventures, and Siegfried describes his youth in the forest with Mime—the forging of the sword—the battle with Fafner—and the death of the treacherous dwarf.

"So Mime won his proper wage," sneers Hagen. Unnoticed by the others, he squeezes an herb into his drinking horn. "Refresh yourself with this wine, my friend," he says, handing the horn to Siegfried.

Again the sinister chords of *Magic* sound, as the hero drinks. Then he goes on with his tale; as his hearers listen in amazement, he tells how

Hagen blows a harsh blast on his horn.

the forest bird guided him to the flaming mountain, how he climbed the rock and found there a sleeping Valkyrie. At last he remembers all.

"My kiss awoke her," he cries passionately, "and Brünnhilde became my bride."

Gunther leaps to his feet in dismay; the vassals stand mute with fear. Suddenly two ravens dart up and fly across the Rhine. "Can you understand their speech?" shouts Hagen, pointing. As Siegfried turns to look, he plunges his spear into the hero's back.

"They have decreed your death!" shrieks the Nibelung son, and once again *Alberich's Curse* thunders forth in triumph. Turning on his heel, Hagen strides off.

Siegfried raises himself unsteadily. "Brünnhilde," he whispers, imagining himself back once more on the mountaintop. "Awaken. See, I have come to break your bonds, beloved. . . ." He sinks back upon his shield—dead.

Night has come. Lifting the hero to their shoulders, the vassals start homeward. *Fate* mutters darkly. Then, as mist rises from the Rhine and fills the glen, the motives of Siegfried's life sound in sorrowful procession, and the *Funeral March* thunders to its awesome climax.

Scene Two. At last the mists part. Gutrune paces the deserted hall, filled with strange dread. Why has Siegfried not returned? Suddenly a horn sounds in the distance, and Hagen's harsh voice rings through the night. Lighted by the glare of torches, the vassals carry in the body of Siegfried. "There is your husband," cries Hagen. "He was slain by a wild boar."

Gutrune throws herself beside the hero. "You have murdered my love," she screams wildly, pushing away her brother, who tries to comfort her.

"The guilt is not mine," Gunther cries. "Hagen slew your husband."

The Nibelung son strides forward defiantly. "Yes, *I* killed him," he shouts. "His falsehood was sworn on my spear. Now I claim the Ring."

"Back!" roars Gunther. "The Ring is mine."

Furious, Hagen rushes at him with drawn sword. The king falls, and Hagen springs to Siegfried's side. But, as he reaches for the Ring, the arm of the dead hero raises itself threateningly. Hagen shrinks back.

In that fearful moment Brünnhilde appears. Advancing with quiet dignity, she bids the vassals build a funeral pyre for the hero on the river bank. The Rhinemaidens have told her everything, and now she realizes that Siegfried was tricked into betraying her. She draws the Ring from his finger and places it on her own.

"Accursed gold!" she exclaims. "I give you back to the Rhine daughters. Let them take their treasure from my ashes."

The pyre is now finished, and Siegfried's body is placed on top. Brünnhilde flings a torch among the logs. "Mount to Valhalla, Loge," she commands. "The end of the gods has come at last."

As the flames dart up, she turns eagerly to Grane, who has been led in. "Let us follow Siegfried," she exults, swinging to the horse's back. Once more the wild cry of the Valkyrie bursts from her lips. Shouting a joyous greeting to Siegfried, she urges her steed into the flames. With a surging roar, the fire leaps heavenward. The hall of the Gibichungs splits asunder, and the waters of the Rhine rush up over their banks, sweeping everything before them. On the crest of the flood swim the Rhinemaidens.

"Back from the Ring!" shrieks Hagen, and plunges madly into the waves after the gold. He is dragged to the bottom.

And now the clouds of smoke clear away. In the sky above the mighty fortress of the gods is aflame, and the motive of *Valhalla* crashes forth for the last time, mingling with the flowing melody of the Rhine daughters. Then the theme of the *Power of Love* soars high above the shattered world of gods and men. Purified by Brünnhilde's sacrifice and cleansed of its curse, the glittering gold lies once more in the silent depths of the Rhine.

"Look inside," whispers Rigoletto to Gilda.

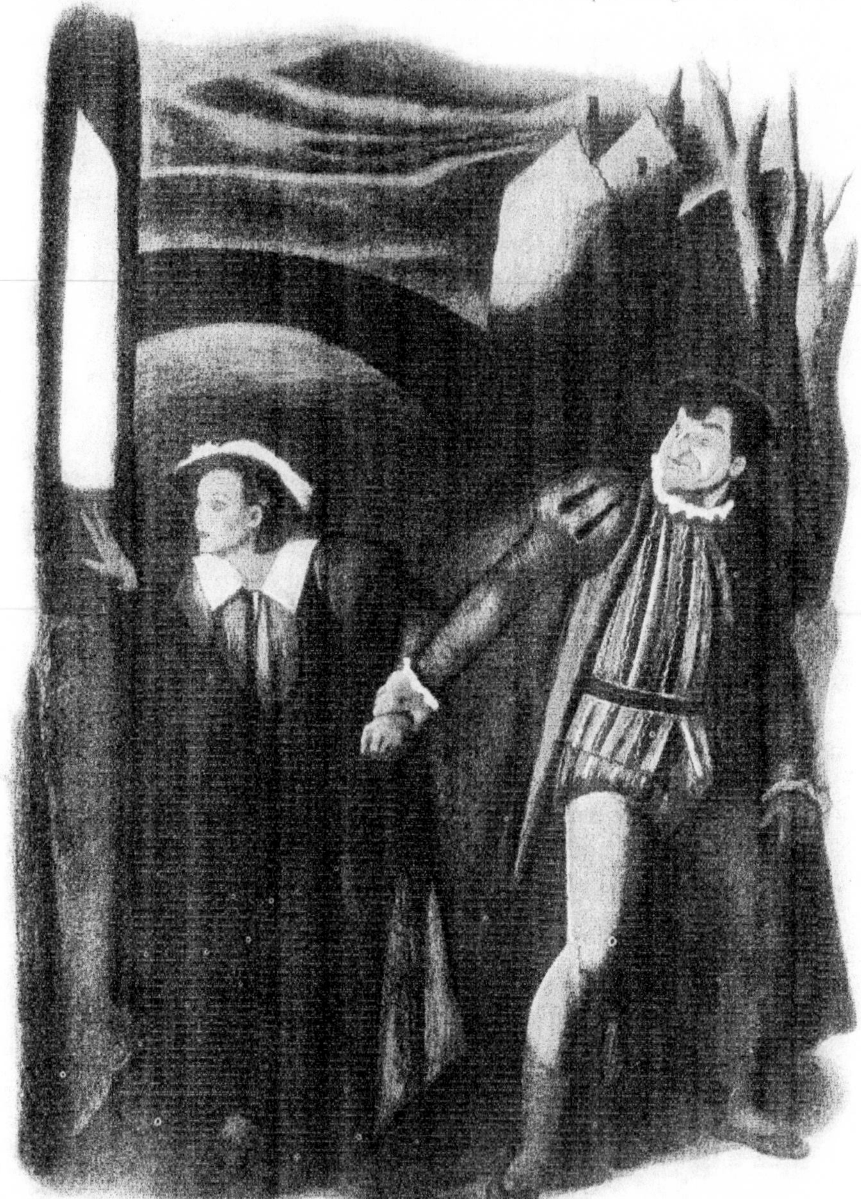

Rigoletto

BY GIUSEPPE VERDI

Libretto by Francesco Maria Piave,
based on Victor Hugo's play, "Le roi s'amuse"

PRINCIPAL CHARACTERS *(in order of appearance):*

The Duke of Mantua (tenor), a handsome young nobleman, who spends his time in revelry and love-making, bestowing his attentions on anyone who pleases him, regardless of the sorrow he causes.

Count Ceprano (bass), a nobleman, with whose beautiful wife the Duke is in love.

Rigoletto (baritone), the Duke's jester, a deformed and ugly hunchback, whose heartless cruelty in aiding the Duke in his many love affairs has made him hated by everyone at court.

Count Monterone (baritone), an elderly nobleman, whose daughter has been betrayed by the Duke.

Sparafucile (bass), an assassin, who keeps a disreputable inn on the outskirts of the city.

Gilda (soprano), Rigoletto's daughter.

Giovanna (mezzo-soprano), Gilda's nurse.

Maddalena (contralto), sister of Sparafucile, who uses her beauty to lure victims to her brother's lonely inn.

PLACE: The city of Mantua, in Italy.   TIME: The sixteenth century.

THE PRELUDE begins with a savage note of vengeance, played softly on the trumpets and trombones, but presently this is swept away by a tune of brilliant, heartless gaiety.

ACT ONE. The curtain rises on a rich apartment in the ducal palace. Cavaliers and their ladies throng the inner rooms, conversing and dancing. The Duke is bragging of his love affairs to a courtier named Borsa.

"It is time I concluded my adventure with the young girl I have been following to church every day," he remarks. Then, noting the Countess Ceprano, he admires her beauty. "My heart has room for them all," he cries blithely.

"One today, another tomorrow. . . ." Nevertheless, he is eager to get the Count out of his way.

"Exile him," councils Rigoletto, making sure that Ceprano hears him. "Or better yet, why not dispose of his head?"

"That stubborn, unbending head," laughs the Duke, tapping the Count on the shoulder.

Rigoletto draws his hand suggestively across his throat. "One stroke," he leers, "and you'll have a new use for it."

"Knave!" shouts Ceprano in a fury. Then, drawing the other courtiers aside, he begs their assistance in avenging himself on the buffoon. "Meet me at midnight," he urges.

The dancers stream out from the inner rooms and at once the crowd turns from thoughts of revenge to revelry. But their merriment is interrupted.

"Make way there," thunders a voice, and an elderly nobleman pushes through the crowd. He pauses haughtily before the Duke. "Yes, it is Monterone, my lord."

Rigoletto anticipates his master's reply. "How now, vassal," he jeers, seating himself on the ducal throne as though giving audience. "Have you come again to threaten me about your daughter's lost honor?"

White with anger, Monterone turns to the Duke. "Is this your justice? Then hear my answer. No place shall ever hide you from my wrath, O Duke. And you, misshapen viper, who mock at a father's deepest anguish. I curse you!" The jester shrinks in horror.

"Away with him, guards," shouts the Duke.

"Begone, disturber of our revels," echoes the crowd, and, as the old man is led away, the courtiers follow the Duke to another chamber.

ACT TWO. Dark night hangs over Mantua. Heavily muffled in a cloak, Rigoletto shuffles cautiously down a deserted street that skirts the high ramparts of the Ceprano palace, then the lower wall of a small court-yard. "He laid a father's curse on me," he mutters, pausing before a doorway in the low wall. Out of the shadows steps a tall stranger.

"You have a wife or maiden in there," he whispers, pointing to the courtyard. "Perhaps you've a rival you'd like to be rid of," and he offers the hunchback the services of his sword.

"Good," answers Rigoletto. "I may need you. Now be off." He looks after Sparafucile as the assassin disappears in the darkness.

"We are alike," he reflects bitterly. "He stabs at night with a sword, I by day with my tongue. . . . O, merciless Fate, that doomed me to a life of deformity, why, why was I born? 'Come, buffoon,' cries my prince, 'make us laugh.' . . . And I must obey. O shame unending, to be forever the butt of scorn and ridicule. I hate you, fawning courtiers," he screams passionately. "If I am vile, you have made me so."

As he turns the latch in the door, Gilda runs from the house to meet him, and Rigoletto embraces her fondly. But he is fearful for her safety. The door of the terrace must never be opened, he tells her; she must never venture out except to go to church. He fancies that he hears some-one in the street and rushes out wildly. A man slips into the garden. Unseen by all excepting the maid, Giovanna, to whom he throws a purse, he conceals himself in the shrubbery.

"Take care you never open to anyone," cautions Rigoletto, return-ing. Then, praying Heaven to watch over his Gilda, the one joy of his life, the old buffoon departs.

Left alone with Giovanna, Gilda is uneasy. Perhaps she should have told her father of the youth who has followed her to church. "I love him," she cries. "If only he loved me."

"He does love you," answers the young man, springing out of hiding.

It is the Duke. "Light of my life," he whispers ardently, "be mine forever." Gilda sinks into his arms. But she longs to know her lover's name.

The Duke thinks quickly.

"I am Walter Maldè," he tells her. "A poor student."

At that moment Giovanna enters, warning of approaching footsteps.

"My father," falters Gilda, and she urges her lover to fly. Hastily they promise to love one another forever, then the Duke slips away. Gilda gazes after him. "Walter Maldè," she repeats softly. "Your name is carved on my heart."

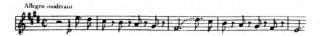

Fetching a lamp from the house, she looks out from the terrace down the long dark alley after her lover. Below, Count Ceprano and his fellow conspirators are gathering outside the house of Rigoletto.

"Who goes there?" challenges a harsh voice in the blackness. It is the jester. Ceprano conceals himself quickly; the others gather around Rigoletto.

"We plan to carry off Ceprano's wife for the Duke," they explain. "Come, join us." Reassured, the buffoon agrees to help, but as his enemies tie on his mask they deftly blindfold him, then set him to holding a ladder under the terrace.

The conspirators swarm into Rigoletto's house. They return with Gilda. The poor girl is gagged, but as her captors carry her, struggling, down the alley, she loosens the scarf from her mouth and calls desperately for her father. "Success," shout the courtiers in the distance.

Suddenly Rigoletto becomes aware of a deep and ominous silence. He tears the bandage from his eyes. There lies Gilda's scarf. Speechless with fear he rushes into the house and drags out the frightened Giovanna. Then, at last, he finds his voice. "Ah, me," he shrieks despairingly. *"It was a father's curse!"*

THE THIRD ACT opens on an antechamber in the palace. On either side of folding doors at the rear are large portraits, one of the Duke, the other of his Duchess. The Duke is bewailing the loss of Gilda, but

his distress is cut short by the courtiers, who enter in haste to tell him
of their exploit. "Not only have we captured the buffoon's sweetheart,"
they declare, "we have brought her here to the palace in order to taunt
Rigoletto when he comes in search of her."

"What," cries the Duke, in delight. "Gilda here?" And he hastens off.

Hardly has he left when Rigoletto is heard approaching. The buffoon
is singing a mocking song. "La-ra, la-ra," he hums, swinging his mottled
jester's scepter with an air of indifference.

But his little eyes dart here and there, hunting desperately for some
sign of his daughter. He finds a handkerchief and hides it quickly. "It
is not hers."

A page enters with a message for the Duke. The courtiers refuse him
admission. Then Rigoletto understands. "She is here with the Duke!"

"Look someplace else for your sweetheart," taunt the courtiers.

But Rigoletto hides his secret no longer. "Give me back my daughter," he cries, trying to push his way through the crowd to the door.
"Yes, my daughter! Have you sold her, whom no gold will buy? Let
me enter, assassins!"

They thrust him back in stony silence.

"O, my lords," weeps the buffoon. "Will no one have pity on a
father's despair?"

Suddenly the door is flung open. Disheveled and frantic, Gilda rushes
out and throws herself into his arms. The jester orders the courtiers
from the room.

When they are alone, Gilda sorrowfully tells him of the Duke's
treachery.

"We must flee from this place," responds Rigoletto. But as they turn
to go, the doors at the rear are opened and Monterone, escorted by
halberdiers, passes through the antechamber on his way to prison. The
aged nobleman pauses an instant before the portrait of the Duke. "My
curse has not brought judgment on you," he exclaims bitterly as he
leaves the room.

Rigoletto leaps to his feet. "*I* will avenge you." With blazing eyes he faces the portrait. "Beware the jester, Duke," he screams. "You will feel the wrath of a father."

Gilda pleads for her lover's life, but the buffoon is beside himself with fury, and vowing vengeance he drags her from the palace.

THE FOURTH ACT curtain rises on a lonely spot on the shores of the Mincio river, not far from Mantua. Here stands the inn of Sparafucile, the assassin. It is night. On the road outside the inn, Rigoletto and Gilda linger in agitated conversation. The girl cannot be convinced of her lover's faithlessness. "Look inside, then," whispers the jester, pointing to a crack in the shuttered window.

Within, Sparafucile is polishing his belt. He is interrupted by a knock on the door, and the Duke enters, dressed in the uniform of a cavalry officer. "Wine," he orders brusquely. Then, seating himself on the table, he sings a gay song about the fickleness of women:

Presently, Maddalena, the lovely sister of Sparafucile, slips into the room. The Duke has been waiting for her, and, springing to his feet, he greets her ardently. She evades his embraces.

"I treasure you above all others," he protests.

But the girl only laughs. "Empty flattery," she retorts.

To Gilda, listening at the window, the Duke's wooing is no idle jest. "Ah, to speak so of love," she whispers, sobbing, for at last she sees her lover in his true colors.

Rigoletto draws her away from the window. "I will avenge you, child," he promises. "Now flee. Disguise yourself as a boy and take horse to Verona at once." Gilda departs reluctantly.

The night has become ominous. Dark clouds are rolling up on the horizon and distant lightning flashes warn of an approaching storm. Rigoletto consults with Sparafucile. "Here is half the money," whispers the jester. "I will return at midnight with the rest, and you will then deliver the victim to me."

Inside, the Duke, all unaware of impending doom, flirts with Maddalena. Finally he bids her goodnight, and, led by Sparafucile, mounts to his chamber, where he carelessly lays aside his sword and hat. The assassin looks at the sword. Then he descends the stairs.

Suddenly a slim figure clad in boy's clothes slips out of the black night below and steals to the window. Fearful for her faithless lover, Gilda has returned, and now listens in horror to the conversation of Sparafucile and his sister. Maddalena pleads for the Duke's life. The stranger is handsome, he has bewitched her heart. Can they not murder the jester himself when he returns, and take his money?

"I am no thief," responds the assassin indignantly. "No, the young man must die unless some wayfarer happens by whom we can substitute for him."

The girl outside makes a quick decision. Breathing a prayer for forgiveness, she steps to the door and knocks. "Who is there?" cries Maddalena, startled.

"A lone wanderer."

Immediately the light in the inn is extinguished. Dagger in hand, Sparafucile slips behind the door, and as Gilda steps across the dark threshold the storm breaks out in savage fury.

Toward midnight the rain ceases. All is silent. Presently Rigoletto shuffles along the road to the inn. "O hour of vengeance," he mutters. "How I have waited for you during all the bitter years. . . ."

In the distance a clock strikes twelve. Sparafucile appears, dragging a sack behind him. He takes Rigoletto's money and vanishes.

The buffoon gazes upon the shapeless bundle in triumph. "There he lies, the proud tyrant," he gloats. "And I, I, the miserable jester, am lord." He seizes the sack to drag it to the river bank.

Suddenly the voice of the duke rings out in the night, singing: "Women are fickle. . . ."

Rigoletto starts up wildly. "Am I mad?" he cries. "The fiend is here, dead." And in an agony of fear he rips open the sack. Gilda lies before him. She moves feebly. "Live, my child," he implores her frantically. "Live for me. O my Gilda, don't leave me here alone." But she lingers only a few minutes. "I will wait for you, father, beyond. . . ."

In despair the buffoon tears his ragged locks. "Lost!" he screams. "Lost forever. . . . *Ah, it was a father's curse!*" He falls senseless on the body of his daughter.

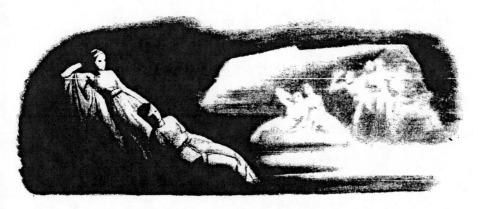

Tannhäuser

BY RICHARD WAGNER

Libretto by the composer, based on an old medieval legend

PRINCIPAL CHARACTERS *(in order of appearance):*

Tannhäuser (tenor), a minstrel knight, whose passionate and quarrelsome nature has led him first into conflict with the knights of the Wartburg, then to seek out Venus.

Venus (soprano), goddess of pagan love, holds her pagan court in the Hörselberg, a mysterious hill near the Wartburg.

Hermann (bass), Landgrave of Thuringia.

Wolfram von Eschenbach (baritone), a noble minstrel knight in the service of the Landgrave. He is deeply in love with the Landgrave's niece, Elizabeth. (Wolfram was a real poet who lived in the thirteenth century.)

Elizabeth (soprano), a lovely, pure-hearted maiden.

PLACE: In Germany, near Eisenach.   TIME: Early thirteenth century.

THE PRELUDE opens with the solemn *Chant of the Pilgrims:*

It swells into a mighty hymn, then begins to fade in the distance. Suddenly its harmonies are shattered by a wild, leaping melody. the motive of the *Venusberg:*

With this melody the orchestra springs into dazzling life. The *Hymn to Venus* bursts out triumphantly:

A hush follows in which the voice of the clarinet and the murmur of strings whisper of *Enchantment:*

Again the music sweeps up, the cymbals clash, and the curtain rises on a vast grotto in the heart of the earth.

ACT ONE, *Scene One.* Here Venus holds her court. The goddess is reclining on a couch with Tannhäuser at her feet, while before her in the soft, rosy light nymphs and fauns whirl in wild dance. But Venus tires of her amusement, and the Three Graces by her side signal the dancers to depart. The voices of sirens are heard in the distance:

At last Venus and her lover are alone.

Tannhäuser rises with a start. "O, that I might wake once more to hear the sound of bells on the summer breeze," he cries softly.

"What folly is this?" exclaims Venus. "Surely you are not tired of the Venusberg." She hands him his harp. "Up, my minstrel! Sing in praise of love, the greatest prize of all."

Tannhäuser seizes the harp and sings a passionate *Hymn to Venus.* "All praise to you, wondrous goddess!" he cries. "You have brought me happiness fit for gods. . . . But alas, I am only a mortal, and I long for life on earth. Will you not set me free?"

"Traitor!" cries Venus, springing to her feet. "You scorn the very love you praise! I shall not let you go." Turning, she points to the

"Stand back!" cries Elizabeth, protecting Tannhäuser with her body.

distant grottos, bathed in mysterious light. "Look, beloved!" she whispers to the strains of *Enchantment*. "Let us forget all these troubled thoughts in new delights."

Again Tannhäuser seizes his harp and praises the beautiful queen of the underworld. He will be her champion, he will defend her name with harp and sword, but she must let him depart.

"Then go!" shrieks Venus furiously. "The world will reject you, and in despair you will return to me."

"Never!" cries Tannhäuser. "My hope is in the Virgin Mary."

Venus shrinks back with a cry of dismay, and in an instant her kingdom is swallowed up in blackness.

Scene Two. Tannhäuser finds himself standing in a sunlit valley near a little wooden shrine of the Virgin. Behind him, on a crag, rises the castle of the Wartburg. Sheep bells are jangling, and the shepherd boy who sits piping on a rocky hillock sings a welcome to the spring.

All at once voices are heard chanting in the distance, and a band of pilgrims trudges through the valley bound for Rome. As they disappear, Tannhäuser sinks to his knees, vowing that he, too, will not rest till he has won pardon for his sins.

Suddenly a horn rings on the heights. It is answered by others, and the Landgrave comes down the path followed by a party of minstrels in hunting dress. They stop short on seeing a stranger bowed in prayer.

"It is Heinrich Tannhäuser!" cries Wolfram, hastening forward.

Tannhäuser leaps to his feet. "Where have you been?" ask the minstrels, crowding around him. "Do you return to us as friend or foe?"

"We meet as friends," he replies. "But my days at the Wartburg are over. Let me go in peace." Despite their protests, he turns away and is about to plunge into the woods when Wolfram calls after him: "Stay for the sake of Elizabeth!" Tannhäuser stops as though bewitched.

Wolfram tells him that his singing at the Wartburg had won him the heart of the Landgrave's niece. "Since you left she has hidden herself from us in grief," says the knight. "Return, and bring her the happiness she has waited for so long."

"Yes, return!" urge the others. Deeply stirred, Tannhäuser consents. "Now the world smiles on me again!" he exclaims.

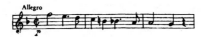

"Oh, guide me to her."

Huntsmen swarm into the glen, and all prepare to mount to the Wartburg.

ACT TWO. The prelude begins with a joyous echo of Tannhäuser's happiness, darkened for a moment by a hint of Venus's warning that the world would reject him. Then the curtain rises on the great hall of the Wartburg.

Elizabeth enters joyously. "I greet you, wonderful hall of song," she cries, gazing about her.

Wolfram appears in the arched doorway at the back with Tannhäuser, who strides forward impetuously and throws himself at her feet.

"Oh, do not kneel," she pleads, "for this hall is your kingdom. You have conquered it with your songs."

Tannhäuser rises slowly. "A miracle of Heaven brought me back to you," he declares.

"Then I prize that miracle with all my heart," cries Elizabeth. and tells him that his songs had awakened emotions she never felt before. "When you left, all joy left too," she says softly. "O Heinrich, what have you done to me?"

"The god of love has united us," he exults, and joyously they bless the hour that brought them together. Then, kissing her hand, he hastens off to prepare for the contest.

He has scarcely disappeared when the Landgrave comes to welcome his niece back to the hall she has deserted for so long.

"All our nobles will be present at the festivities today," he tells her, "for they know that your hand will again crown the victor."

A fanfare interrupts him, and, mounting their thrones, the Landgrave and Elizabeth greet the knights and ladies as they are escorted to their seats by the heralds.

Last of all come the minstrels. Bowing to the assembly, they take their places in the center of the hall.

Landgrave Hermann rises solemnly. "The minstrel s art has often glorified our land," he begins. "Today we hold yet another song contest, to which we gladly welcome our long-absent singer. His return is still a mystery, but perhaps he will explain it in song. The theme I have chosen is *Love*. So tune your harps, my gallant minstrels, and let us know your thoughts."

His speech is greeted by cheers. As all seat themselves, the pages present Elizabeth with a goblet containing the names of the singers. She chooses one: Wolfram von Eschenbach shall begin the contest.

The minstrel knight rises thoughtfully, and, after saluting his listeners, he turns in quiet devotion to Elizabeth. "I raise my eyes to a distant star," he sings softly. "O, never shall I trouble that pure spirit with my desires, but rather spend my life in worshipping her from afar."

He seats himself amid applause. Tannhäuser has listened as though in a dream, but now, as a hint of the *Venusberg* music leaps upward in the orchestra, he starts to his feet.

"I, too, have known the joy of love, Wolfram," he cries, sweeping the strings of his harp restlessly, "but my heart is not cold like yours. I must approach the flame of love until I am burned by its splendor."

"Your words are an insult to womanhood," shouts an elderly minstrel named Biterolf. "True love is an ideal to be held in reverence."

Tannhäuser laughs. "What can you know of true love, old wolf?"

Enraged, Biterolf draws his sword, and the knights leap up in anger. But the Landgrave orders them to sheathe their weapons. Again Wolfram rises. At once the hall is silent and all listen in rapt attention as the minstrel sings a beautiful song in praise of love.

Tannhäuser starts up in wild excitement. "All praise to you, wondrous goddess of love," he cries, bursting into the *Hymn to Venus,* and turns to his horrified listeners with blazing eyes. "Wretched mortals! You, who have never tasted divine joy! If you want to know the real meaning of love, go to the Venusberg."

The ladies flee from the hall, and, drawing away from Tannhäuser, the men gather about the Landgrave. "His own lips have condemned him," they mutter. "He must die." But as they surge forward with drawn swords, Elizabeth, who has been standing pale as death at one side, rushes between them.

"Stand back!" she cries, protecting Tannhäuser with her body. "Will you deny him all hope of salvation? Ah, what has he done to you? It is I, who love him, whom he has crushed, and I plead for his life."

Overcome with remorse, Tannhäuser sinks to his knees. "O, Thou, who hast sent this angel to pray for me," he implores, "have mercy on my sinful soul." Minstrels and knights join in his prayer.

"You are banished from this domain," the Landgrave tells Tanhäuser, "but there is a way to redemption. Join the pilgrims who are gathering in the valley and go with them to Rome to seek forgiveness."

From the distance comes the chant of the pilgrims. A ray of hope lights Tannhäuser's face. "To Rome!" he cries, and, kissing the hem of Elizabeth's robe, he rushes from the hall.

"To Rome!" Elizabeth and the knights call after him.

ACT THREE. The song of the pilgrims sounds wearily, as though describing their journey along the dusty roads to Rome. Again and again it is interrupted—by the strains of Elizabeth's prayer in behalf of Tannhäuser, and by a mournful phrase suggesting *Penitence:*

Then a new motive, known as *Heavenly Grace,* rings out.

The curtain rises on the valley below the Wartburg. It is autumn and the last rays of the setting sun fall upon Elizabeth, who kneels before the shrine in prayer.

Wolfram comes down the path, but stops when he sees her. "She prays for him night and day," he says softly. "O, may he be with the pilgrims when they return." As he turns to leave, the chant of voices sounds in the distance.

Elizabeth hears it too, and rises. "The pilgrims!" she whispers.

Nearer and nearer comes the chant until at last the singers burst from the woods and stride down the path, bowing to the shrine as they pass. "Hallelujah!" they cry exultantly. "All praise be Thine, O Lord, whose mercy has forgiven us."

Elizabeth scans each face anxiously. *He* is not among them. The pilgrims' voices die away, and again she kneels before the shrine.

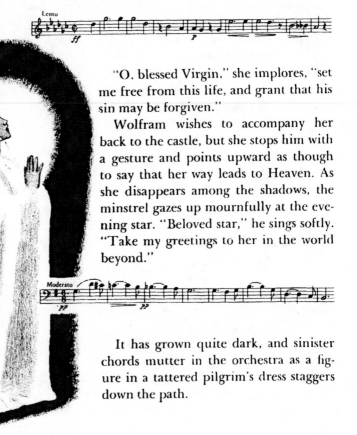

"O, blessed Virgin," she implores, "set me free from this life, and grant that his sin may be forgiven."

Wolfram wishes to accompany her back to the castle, but she stops him with a gesture and points upward as though to say that her way leads to Heaven. As she disappears among the shadows, the minstrel gazes up mournfully at the evening star. "Beloved star," he sings softly. "Take my greetings to her in the world beyond."

It has grown quite dark, and sinister chords mutter in the orchestra as a figure in a tattered pilgrim's dress staggers down the path.

"Heinrich!" exclaims Wolfram, starting forward. "How is it that you come alone? Surely you have not dared to return to us unforgiven."

"Have no fear," answers Tannhäuser harshly. "I am not seeking you or any of your proud companions. I am looking for the Venusberg!"

Horrified, Wolfram asks whether he has been to Rome.

Tannhäuser sits down wearily on a rock. "Yes. I have been to Rome," he replies bitterly. "Ah, no sinner ever yearned for pardon as I yearned, no pilgrim ever suffered more hardships. And when at last we came to Rome, I confessed my crime with repentant tears, imploring the Holy Father to have mercy on me. This is what he said: 'If you have been to the Venusberg you are lost forever. Just as this staff of mine shall never have leaves again, so you shall never know salvation.' "

The sinister chords heard before thunder forth the fearful *Condemnation* of the Pope, and in despair Tannhäuser leaps to his feet. "Men have spurned me," he shrieks. "Now I seek you again, O Venus."

Black clouds have rolled up the valley, and now they begin to glow with rosy light. The music of the *Venusberg* crashes about the ears of the frantic man. Then the siren call sounds, and in the gleaming cloud Venus herself appears. Tannhäuser tears himself madly away from Wolfram and staggers toward her. But his friend seizes him.

"An angel pleads for you in Heaven!" he cries. "Elizabeth!"

At that name Tannhäuser stands rooted to the spot; Venus vanishes with a shriek. Suddenly the night is lighted up by the gleam of torches as a sorrowful procession descends into the valley carrying the body of Elizabeth. Tannhäuser falls on his knees beside her.

"O holy Elizabeth, pray for me," he whispers, and sinks down dead.

The knights and pilgrims put out their torches. Daylight floods the world.

But now a group of young pilgrims rush up the valley. "Behold!" they shout, waving aloft the Pope's staff, on which leaves have broken forth "A miracle! Tannhäuser is forgiven." All sink to their knees, and, as they lift their voices in exultation, the curtain falls.

La Traviata

(THE STRAYED ONE)

BY GIUSEPPE VERDI

Libretto by Francesco Maria Piave
after Dumas' play, "Camille"

PRINCIPAL CHARACTERS *(in order of appearance):*

Violetta Valery (soprano), a beautiful young woman, who has been leading a life of wild gaiety in the salons of Paris.

Flora Bervoix (mezzo-soprano), her friend, a lady of wealth and fashion.

Baron Douphol (bass), a haughty aristocrat, in love with Violetta.

Gastone de Letorieres (tenor), another friend of Violetta and Flora.

Alfredo Germont (tenor), a young man from Provence.

Giorgio Germont (baritone), his father.

PLACE: Paris and vicinity.   TIME: About 1850.

ACT ONE. A soft, mournful melody begins the prelude, hinting that sorrow and tragedy lurk even amid the whirl of Parisian life.

Then follows another beautiful theme, describing the deep love of Violetta for the man to whom she gives her heart.

The curtain rises on a salon in her house in Paris. Violetta is seated on a sofa, surrounded by a group of admirers. She is a delicate woman, and the glittering jewels with which she has adorned herself only emphasize the pallor of her cheeks and the unnatural brightness of her eyes. Flora Bervoix comes in on the arm of the Marquis d'Obigny.

"Do you really enjoy all this excitement, my dear?" she asks Violetta.

"Yes, indeed," the young woman answers gaily. "Pleasure is the best drug for my illness."

Gastone has arrived with a handsome stranger, whom he now introduces to Violetta as Alfredo Germont—an ardent admirer of hers. She gives the young man her hand to kiss. Then, as the banquet is ready, all sit down, Violetta between Gastone and the stranger.

"My friend worships you." Gastone whispers to Violetta. "When you were sick, he came every day to ask for you."

"Is that true, monsieur?" she asks Alfredo. "Then I thank you." She glances across the table. "You, dear Baron, were not so devoted." Baron Douphol glowers jealously, and, laughing, Violetta fills Alfredo's glass.

"A toast!" call the guests. Alfredo leaps to his feet. "Let us drink to pleasure and love," he cries gallantly.

He sings a spirited drinking song, and the others join in gaily.

As the song comes to an end, a waltz is heard in another room, and the company hastens off to join the dancers. At the door, Violetta staggers. "What is it?" cry her friends in alarm. Returning, Violetta sits down on the sofa. "Pray go on without me," she urges, trying to speak lightly. "It is nothing. I will join you in a moment."

All go into the other room except Alfredo, who remains unnoticed at the back. Violetta takes up a small hand mirror and stares at her white face in the glass. Then a movement catches her eye, and, turning, she sees Alfredo. "What, you here!" she exclaims in some annoyance.

He comes forward anxiously. "Are you better now? Ah. Violetta, this life will kill you. If you were mine, how I would care for you!"

She laughs mockingly. "So you really love me?"

"I have loved you for a year," he answers passionately. "To win you is the goal of my life."

The sincerity of his words startles her. "If this is true, you must leave me," she cries hastily. "I must be frank. . . . Love is not for me."

The young man turns away gloomily. Violetta hesitates. Perhaps he really does love her. "Here, take this flower," she says softly. unfastening a blossom from her dress. "Bring it back when it is faded."

Alfredo seizes the flower in wild joy. "I love you," he cries. "Till tomorrow, dearest." and. kissing her hand. he hastens off.

The guests return from the ballroom and take leave of Violetta. She stares after them. "Can it be that I have found the man of my dreams?" she whispers at last,

and softly repeats Alfredo's words of love. . . . "But no, this is folly," she cries. "In gay, heartless Paris there is no room for true love. I will forget my loneliness in pleasure. . . ."

From beneath her window the voice of Alfredo floats up, rapturously singing of his love. Violetta listens, breathless.

ACT TWO. For three months Violetta and Alfredo have been living quietly in a secluded villa near Paris. Returning from a hunt, the young man pauses to rest in the garden. "Violetta has given up all her old pleasures for me," he reflects proudly. "Since she gave me her love, we have lived only for each other."

But his joy is brought to a sudden end. Dressed in travelling clothes, Violetta's maid, Annina, enters hastily, and Alfredo learns to his horror that she has been in Paris attending to the sale of Violetta's possessions, which are being sacrificed to pay for the villa. "How could I have let such a thing happen?" he cries wildly, and rushes off to Paris.

Scarcely has he left when Violetta comes in. Annina tells her that Alfredo has gone to the city. "That is strange," Violetta remarks, opening a letter she has in her hand. It is an invitation from Flora to a dance that night. She tosses it aside. "Those days are over!" she exclaims.

A visitor is announced. Violetta has been expecting her business agent and is astonished when an elderly gentleman comes forward and introduces himself as Alfredo's father. "You are leading my son to ruin," he declares angrily. "He is spending his entire fortune on you."

Violetta turns to him with quiet dignity. "You are mistaken," she says. "Alfredo has not offered to spend his fortune on me, and if he did I would not allow it." She shows him the papers disposing of her possessions. "I love Alfredo," she cries. "Heaven has forgiven my sins."

"That may be," Germont answers. "But you are known everywhere for the wild life you have led, and I must ask you to break off your friendship with him. His whole future is at stake, and his sister will not be able to marry unless you free my family of this disgrace."

"How can I give him up?" cries Violetta in despair. "You do not know how I love him."

Germont is moved by her sorrow, but he is determined to have his way. "Some day Alfredo may get tired of you," he suggests. "Then you will have no one. Better to make new friendships now.

Grief-stricken, the girl agrees to do as he wishes. Asking Germont to wait in the garden, she sits down and dashes off an acceptance to Flora. Writing to Alfredo is harder. She has barely sealed the letter when her lover appears.

She tells him that his father is coming to visit them. He is disturbed by the news, but tries to persuade himself that the old man will approve of Violetta when he sees her.

"No, no, he must not see me," she cries wildly. "I'll wait in the garden while you talk to him. . . . O, Alfredo, say that you love me as I love you!" With a sob she hastens off.

He looks after her tenderly. A few minutes later a messenger brings him a note. It is from Violetta; filled with strange dread, he tears it open. . . . With a cry of anguish, he falls into the arms of his father who has hastened from his place of concealment.

The old man tries to comfort his son with childhood memories:

But the young man thrusts him away.

"So she has gone back to her old life," he mutters in fury. Suddenly he sees Flora's letter lying open upon the table and snatches it up. "She's gone to the dance! Well, I'll go too and have my revenge!"

ACT THREE. Flora's guests have gathered on a terrace of her villa. "Violetta and Alfredo are coming tonight," the hostess announces gaily.

"Why, haven't you heard the news?" asks the Marquis. "They have broken up their friendship." Before the others can reply, gypsy entertainers appear and begin to tell the fortunes of the guests. After them come a crowd of maskers dressed as bullfighters.

Alfredo strides in. Flora and the others gather about him, asking after Violetta, but, responding with a shrug, he joins the card players.

A minute later Violetta appears, leaning on the arm of Baron Douphol. "Young Germont is here," he whispers. "Not a word to him, remember." She nods miserably.

Flora draws her down on the sofa, but their conversation is interrupted by noise from the gaming tables. Playing recklessly, Alfredo wins every hand. "Unlucky in love, lucky at cards!" he boasts loudly. "Well, with my winnings I'll soon go back to the country. Only I must find someone to take the place of the one who deserted me."

Angrily the Baron challenges him to a match. Again Alfredo wins.

At that moment a servant announces that supper is ready, and the players rise. "I'll take my revenge another time," the Baron says grimly. "Whenever it suits you," retorts Alfredo as they leave the room.

Violetta returns breathlessly, followed by Alfredo. "I sent for you to beg you to leave," she implores. "The Baron is about to challenge you to a duel, Alfredo. You must go at once."

"Only if you come with me," he cries passionately.

"No, I cannot," she answers. "I have sworn never to see you again."

"Who dared ask you? The Baron?"

With a terrible effort Violetta conceals the truth. "Yes," she gasps.

Alfredo runs furiously to the doors and throws them open. "Come here, all of you," he shouts, and, as the guests enter in confusion, he points at Violetta, who leans deathly pale against the table. "There stands the woman whom I basely allowed to spend all her wealth on me," he rages. "But now I redeem myself. Bear witness, everyone, that I pay back the debt." He hurls a purse at the feet of the fainting girl.

The elder Germont has come in just in time to hear his son's violent speech, and joins the others in reproaching him for his insulting conduct. Alfredo is overcome with remorse.

"O, my love," whispers Violetta, "some day you will know of the sacrifice that brought about all this woe."

ACT FOUR. The mournful theme heard in the beginning of the opera sounds again, swelling and dying away like the sigh of a broken heart. Then the curtain rises on a darkened bedroom in a Parisian apartment. Violetta lies in bed, asleep. Beside her on the table are medicines, and her maid, Annina, drowses in a near-by chair.

At last Violetta stirs. "Annina," she calls weakly.

Annina opens the blinds. "Doctor Grenvil is coming," she tells her mistress. Violetta tries to

rise, but she is too weak, and the doctor enters in time to help her to the lounge.

"Keep up your courage," he says gently. "You will soon be better."

But Violetta shakes her head. She knows very well that she has not much longer to live. The doctor takes his leave, whispering to Annina at the door that the end is only a few hours away, and, anxious to be alone, Violetta sends the maid out to give money to the poor.

The music of Alfredo's love song steals through the orchestra as she takes out a crumpled letter and begins to read: "The duel between the Baron and Alfredo has taken place. The Baron was wounded. I have told Alfredo of your sacrifice and we are both coming to beg your forgiveness. . . . Giorgio Germont."

Violetta rises. "They will come too late!" she cries despairingly. A mirror lies at hand. Taking it up, she stares at her pallid face. "How changed I am," she murmurs. "Ah, farewell bright days when I dreamed that I, too, might have happiness. . . ."

From the street outside the gay song of a carnival crowd drifts up like an echo out of the past. Violetta listens forlornly. Suddenly Annina rushes in with the news that Alfredo is coming, and a minute later the young man bursts into the room. The lovers fall into each other's arms. Nothing will ever separate them again.

Alfredo begs Violetta to fly with him from Paris to find a new life of happiness far away:

She consents joyously. But suddenly she staggers and sinks down on a chair.

Terrified, Alfredo sends Annina for the doctor.

"It is nothing," murmurs Violetta. Struggling against the overpowering weakness that has come over her, she tries to put on her shawl. But she cannot. "Ah, my dearest," she whispers to Alfredo. "If your coming cannot save me, no power on earth can do so." She starts to her feet, wildly imploring Heaven not to let her die now, when happiness has come to her at last. Again she staggers, and Alfredo helps her to the lounge.

The elder Germont hastens in, eager to unite her with his son. "You are too late," she whispers. Taking a miniature from a drawer, she gives it to Alfredo. "Keep this to remind you of me," she says softly. "And if you should marry, tell your bride that I am praying for you both."

Annina returns with the doctor, but, before he can reach her side, Violetta sways to her feet. "The pain . . . has gone," she gasps, her face radiant. "O. Alfredo . . . it is life . . . coming back. . . ." With a last rapturous cry, she sinks back on the sofa—dead.

"Let us drink to pleasure and love!"

Tristan und Isolde

BY RICHARD WAGNER

Libretto by the composer

PRINCIPAL CHARACTERS *(in order of appearance):*

Isolde (soprano), beautiful young Irish princess.

Brangäne (mezzo-soprano), her maid.

Kurvenal (baritone), rough but loyal servingman to Tristan.

Tristan (tenor), renowned knight of Brittany, and nephew of the king of Cornwall, who has gone to Ireland to fetch Isolde to be his uncle's bride.

Melot (tenor), a knight of Cornwall and friend of Tristan.

King Marke (bass), the elderly king of Cornwall.

PLACE: Cornwall and Brittany.   TIME: Legendary.

THE PRELUDE begins with a short, pleading melody, whispered in the stillness like a *Confession of Love*. It merges into a second melody that seems to express the longing and *Desire* of lovers to be with one another:

Again and again the motives sound. Then a new and beautiful theme is heard on the 'cellos. It describes the *Glance*—that fateful glance when Tristan and Isolde looked deep into each other's eyes back in Ireland and fell in love:

Surging through the orchestra with the other motives it tells of their joys and sorrows. Suddenly a rushing sweep on the strings sings of *Deliverance by Death:*

All the motives cry out in an agonizing climax, then die away abruptly, and, as at the beginning, only the sighs of the lovers break the silence.

ACT ONE. The curtain rises on the deck of Tristan's ship, at sea between Ireland and Cornwall. Within a richly hung pavilion lies Isolde, her face buried in the pillows of her couch. The voice of a sailor drifts down from the masthead: "Is it your sighs that fill the sails, my lovely Irish maid?"

Isolde starts up. "Who dares to mock me?" she wonders. She looks around uneasily, and, catching sight of Brangäne at the ship's side, asks where they are.

"If the sea remains calm we will surely reach Cornwall by evening," the maid replies.

"Never!" cries Isolde, springing to her feet in wild despair. "O Mother, where is your mighty witchcraft that can command the seas? Up, winds! Up, waves! Hear my will and shatter this insolent ship."

Filled with alarm, Brangäne leads the distracted princess back to the couch. She has feared this outburst ever since they left Ireland, for day after day Isolde has sat, pale and silent, refusing either to eat or to sleep. "Will you not tell me what is troubling you?" implores the maid.

In answer Isolde calls for air. Brangäne draws up the great curtains at the back, and now the lofty afterdeck is seen, crowded with sailors and knights. Tristan stands at the helm.

Isolde stares up at him. "Must I lose the one I have chosen?" she whispers. "Then let me find release in *Death*."

She laughs harshly. "What do you think of the hero up yonder who hides his eyes from me in shame?" she asks Brangäne. "Go to the proud knave and tell him that I. Isolde, command him to come to me."

Fearfully Brangäne makes her way up, and begs Tristan to go to her mistress.

The knight is reluctant to obey. "If I leave the helm, how can I pilot the ship safely to King Marke?" he asks.

"Your lordship is mocking me," replies the maid. "My mistress bade me tell you that she, Isolde, commands you to come to her."

Kurvenal, who has been sitting at Tristan's feet, leaps up. "Let me answer that," he cries roughly, and bursts into a mocking ballad about the Irish champion, Sir Morold, who had come to collect a tax from Cornwall. "Instead he got his death-wound from Tristan," he taunts, "and his head was sent back to Ireland. Hail to our lord, Tristan. He knows how to pay a tax!"

Brangäne flees in dismay, and, laughing, the crew takes up the chant.

Isolde springs to her feet, her eyes flashing dangerously. "Well, what of Tristan?" she demands, as Brangäne closes the curtain.

"He says he must pilot the ship to King Marke," wails the maid.

"Ah, yes." Isolde retorts bitterly. "To pay over to his uncle the bride he has collected as a tax from Ireland! Now you know my shame. Listen to what brought it upon me." She tells her maid of the desperately wounded man who came to Ireland in a small boat after Morold's death.

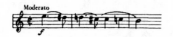

"My skill healed him," she declares. "But one day I discovered a nick in the blade of his sword that fitted the splinter taken from Morold's wound. Then I knew that the man who called himself Tantris was none other than Tristan, and I resolved to slay him in vengeance. But he looked up into my eyes . . . and the sword fell from my hand. Now the man whom I saved by my silence returns in force to demand the hand of Ireland's heiress for his old uncle, once a vassal of the Irish throne. If Morold were alive nobody would have dared offer us such an insult." In despairing fury she rushes back to the curtain. "Curses upon you, dastard! Vengeance! May death come to us both."

Brangäne tries to comfort her. "Surely there is no better way that Tristan could repay you for your mercy than by making you queen of Cornwall," she cries.

Isolde turns away gloomily. "How can I bear to be always near him and yet unloved?" she mutters. Brangäne thinks she means the king.

"Who could help loving you?" she exclaims. "But if your lover grows cold, you can win him back with your mother's potions."

"I have not forgotten my mother's art," Isolde answers. "Bring me the casket."

The maid fetches a golden box and points out the love potion. Isolde thrusts it aside. "This is the drink that will serve me best," she cries, holding up a black phial.

Brangäne recoils in horror. "The death potion!" she screams.

Entering abruptly, Kurvenal bids the women make ready to land.

Isolde turns to him with quiet dignity. "Take my greetings to Sir Tristan," she says. "But tell him that before I go with him to meet his master, he must seek my forgiveness for the wrong he has done me."

Kurvenal leaves with the message, and Isolde commands Brangäne to prepare the death potion. "For whom?" cries the maid in terror.

"For him who betrayed me!"

Kurvenal announces Tristan. Controlling herself with an effort, Isolde turns as the motive of *Tristan the Hero* thunders forth:

Tristan seizes the cup
Isolde holds out to him.

"Why have you scorned my summons?" she demands.

Tristan replies that the customs of his country require that the bride-bringer must stay away from the bride.

Angrily. Isolde reminds him that it is also a custom to settle blood-feuds, and demands vengeance for the death of her fiancé, Sir Morold.

Pale and gloomy, Tristan offers her his sword. "If Morold was so dear to you." he replies, "take my sword again. But this time do not fail."

Isolde waves the weapon aside. "What would King Marke say if I slew his best vassal?" she taunts. "No, my lord. Put away your sword and let us drink a truce together." She signals Brangäne to prepare the draught. The maid hesitates, then quickly pours one of the potions into a goblet.

The shouts of the sailors in the rigging warn that the voyage is over. Tristan seizes the cup Isolde holds out to him, aware that it is poison. "To Tristan's honor!" he cries. "May I forget my sorrows in oblivion!" But as he drinks Isolde snatches the cup from him.

"Leave half for me," she cries. "Betrayer, I drink to you!"

The empty cup falls from her hands. Motionless, the lovers wait for death. Then suddenly a trembling seizes them. They stare at one another passionately, and as the love themes steal through the orchestra Isolde whispers his name. "Beloved!" he answers, and sweeps her into his arms.

Outside the sailors shout a welcome to the king. Starting up, Brangäne sees her mistress in Tristan's arms and wrings her hands in horror. But the lovers are oblivious of everything except each other. Again the curtains of the pavilion are raised, and, approaching his master, Kurvenal tells him that the king is about to come on board.

"What king?" shouts Tristan, and Kurvenal falls back in dismay.

Faintly Isolde remembers that she had sought death. "Where am I?" she asks Brangäne. "Ah, what drink did you give us?"

"The love draught," wails the maid.

Isolde gazes at Tristan in terror. "Must I live?" she gasps, and sinks. half-fainting, on his breast. As men from the shore climb aboard, the curtain falls swiftly.

ACT TWO. The harsh theme of *Day* blares out like a threat:

Then the murmuring of *Night* is heard, and melodies describing

Isolde's *Impatient Longing* to see her lover rush through the orchestra:

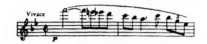

The curtain rises on a shadowy garden outside the castle of King Marke. On the terrace a torch burns brightly.

Brangäne stands on the steps of the tower. "I still hear the hunting horns," she says as Isolde comes out, and warns her mistress that Melot has arranged the hunt so that the king can discover her with Tristan.

Isolde laughs at her fears. "Melot is a better friend than you are," she exclaims, "for he does not try to prevent me from seeing Tristan. Put out the torch, Brangäne. I hear nothing but rustling leaves."

"Leave the warning light," implores the maid, and blames herself bitterly for having caused all this woe by changing the potions.

"It was not your work, foolish maid!" cries Isolde. "The Goddess of Love decides our destinies, and she now commands me to put out the light." Seizing the torch, she dashes it to the ground.

Brangäne goes up to keep watch in the tower. Climbing halfway up the steps, Isolde gazes eagerly into the night. What can be delaying Tristan? She waves her scarf impatiently to urge him to hurry, and at last he springs up the garden path. In a moment they are in each other's arms.

"How long I waited for the hateful torch to disappear," he cries.

"My maid refused to put it out," answers Isolde. "But love defied the envious light!"

"Then let darkness surround us. . . ." Gently, Tristan draws her to a bench below the terrace. About them the garden murmurs softly, and lifting their voices they implore the mystic night to set them free of the world of day that separates them from each other:

From the tower above floats the watch song of Brangäne, warning them to be careful.

"Listen, dearest," whispers Isolde.

Tristan will not listen. "If we were both to die," he tells her, "then we would never be parted."

Again Brangäne sings her song of warning. But now the lovers are absorbed in their new dream of never being parted. Springing to their feet, they come forward, and their voices soar higher and higher as they sing a passionate *Hymn to Death.* . . .

Suddenly a shriek rings out.

"Save yourself, Tristan!" shouts Kurvenal, rushing in with drawn sword. A moment later Melot appears, followed by the king and his hunting party. Instinctively Tristan tries to hide Isolde by raising his cloak. It is too late. The theme of *Day* echoes in the orchestra, and slowly the cold gray light of dawn floods the world.

Melot turns to the king. "I told you we would find him here," he boasts.

The aging monarch gazes sadly at his nephew. "How could you repay my love with such treachery?" he reproaches. "It was only because you threatened to leave my court if I didn't remarry that I agreed to let you woo Isolde for me. Now you, yourself, have shattered my happiness, and forced me to lurk in the night like a common spy. Why must I suffer such shame? Who will explain the mystery of your actions?"

"O, King," replies Tristan sadly, "I can never answer your question." He turns to Isolde and tells her that he must now go away to a far land.

"It is the land of night," he says gently. "Will you follow me there?"

She looks up at him trustingly. "Once before I followed you to a strange country," she whispers. "Shall I not go with you now?"

He bends down and kisses her softly on the brow. Melot starts forward with a cry of rage, and Tristan turns to face him.

"This was my friend," he cries bitterly. "But your beauty blinded him too, Isolde, and in jealousy he betrayed me." Tristan rushes at his enemy with drawn sword, but does not try to protect himself; Melot's blade pierces his unguarded breast.

ACT THREE. The sea thunders with a hollow roar against the cliffs of Brittany, and like an echo empty chords rise upward, suggesting the *Solitude* of the bleak coast. Mournfully, the motive of *Tristan's Anguish* sounds above the pounding surf:

Then the curtain rises on the courtyard of a half-ruined castle by the sea.

Tristan lies stretched on a couch under a lime-tree, tended by Kurvenal, who listens anxiously to the faint breathing of the wounded man.

Beyond the sea wall an old shepherd is playing a dreary tune on his pipe:

At last he looks over the wall. "Kurvenal," he whispers, "has he wakened yet?"

"No," laments the squire. "But if you see a sail, play a joyful tune to let me know that help is coming."

The shepherd turns away and again the mournful sound of his piping is heard.

Tristan stirs. "Where am I?" he asks weakly.

Overjoyed, Kurvenal throws himself down beside the couch. "You are in your own castle of Kareol, my lord," he cries. "Here you will soon get well."

"You are wrong," answers Tristan. "I came from the realm of night and death and long to return to it. But Isolde is still alive, and so I cannot die. Ah. beloved. when will you come to set me free?"

"She will come today," Kurvenal declares. "I have sent for her."

Tristan struggles to his knees in wild joy. "Truest of friends," he gasps, "how can I thank you—you who share every joy and sorrow with me except the longing that burns my heart? If you felt that, you would rush to the watchtower to look for her sail." He imagines he sees the ship approaching. "She is past the reef." he shouts. "Kurvenal, can't you see her?"

In answer, the mournful tune of the shepherd drifts up from below.

"Is that the meaning of the old song?" cries Tristan despairingly. "Am I condemned to endless longing? O, I curse you, terrible love potion!" He falls back unconscious.

Kurvenal bends over him in terror. fearing that he is dead. But no, his heart still beats. Tristan opens his eyes wearily, and to comfort him the old retainer promises that the ship will surely come today.

"And bring Isolde to me." whispers the dying man. As in a dream, he fancies he sees her coming to him across the water. "Ah, Isolde, how beautiful you are!" But why can't Kurvenal see her? "Quick, up to the watchtower." he cries impatiently.

The squire hesitates. Suddenly a joyous melody sounds on the shepherd's pipe. "The ship!" Kurvenal cries, rushing to the battlements. "There she comes," he shouts, and races down to the shore to meet Isolde.

Tristan tosses on his couch in feverish excitement. At last he can wait no longer. and staggers to his feet. Ripping open his shirt, he tears the bandages from his wound. "Isolde will cure me," he cries.

From without comes a cry: "Tristan, beloved!" and, rushing up the path, Isolde catches him in her arms. Once again they gaze deep into each other's eyes. "Isolde!" he whispers, and sinks back on the couch —dead.

She bends over him in wild grief. "It is I. beloved," she pleads desperately. "Hear me this one last time! How many weary hours I waited in longing to live just one more hour with you. How joyfully I came to you over the sea. Too late!" She sinks fainting beside him.

Kurvenal has been watching in horror. Now the shepherd calls to him that another ship has come bearing King Marke and his men, and, seizing his sword, the old retainer rushes furiously into the fray. He strikes down Melot, but the odds against him are too great. Mortally wounded, he drags himself to the couch and falls dead at Tristan's feet.

The king and his followers burst into the courtyard, then stop in dismay at the sight that greets them.

Brangäne hastens to Isolde and at last revives her. "Dearest mistress," she cries, "I told the king about the love potion, and he has come to unite you with Tristan."

Marke echoes her story. But Isolde does not hear them. "How gently he is smiling," she whispers, gazing at Tristan, and her voice rises in the beautiful melody of the *Hymn to Death* that she and Tristan sang in the garden. Now it has become the *Liebestod,* or *Love Death.* Isolde's voice soars ever higher: "See, how his spirit is borne to the stars. Ah, does no one else hear the wondrous music that weaves about him, leading us to a dreamless sleep?" Transfigured, she sinks down beside Tristan. As the last rays of the setting sun fall upon the lovers, Marke lifts his hand in blessing.

Il Trovatore
(THE TROUBADOUR)

BY GIUSEPPE VERDI

Libretto by Cammanaro

PRINCIPAL CHARACTERS *(in order of appearance):*

Ferrando (bass), captain of the guard, in the service of Count di Luna.
Leonora (soprano), beautiful young lady-in-waiting to the Queen of Aragon.
The Count di Luna (baritone), fierce and vengeful nobleman of Aragon.
Manrico (tenor), a young knight.
Azucena (mezzo-soprano), a wild gypsy, who has raised him as her son.
PLACE: Aragon, and the mountain of Biscay, Spain.   TIME: The fifteenth century.

ACT ONE, *Scene One.* Trumpets sound a fanfare, setting a mood of medieval chivalry. After a pause it rings out again, but this time far away, and the last notes merge into an ominous chord as though foretelling some terrible fate.

The curtain rises on a hall in the palace of Aliaferia. It is almost midnight, and a group of servants and soldiers of Count di Luna are slouched on benches along the walls. overcome with weariness. "Bestir yourselves," commands Ferrando. "The count will soon pass this way bound for his nightly vigil beneath the window of his lady."

"They say he is a jealous lover," some of the men remark.

"Well, and why not?" retorts Ferrando. "He has good cause to fear the unknown troubadour who sings in the garden every night."

The men gather around the captain. "Come, help us while away the hours of the watch, Ferrando. Tell us the story of the count's brother."

The captain is glad to oblige. "Once, years ago," he begins,

"the nurse who watched the count's little brother, Garzia, woke at dawn to see a swarthy gypsy bending over the baby. The attendants drove the woman off, but from that day the child began to waste away. In revenge we burned the old witch at the stake, not heeding the threats of her daughter. When we returned to the castle the baby was gone. We searched everywhere, and at last, in the ashes of the gypsy's funeral pyre, we found the remains of a little child."

The listeners gasp in horror. "Did you catch the murderess?" they ask.

"No," answers Ferrando. "She vanished away, and for years we have sought her in vain. But I would recognize her if I saw her again."

"It is said that men have seen an old gypsy riding through the air," the soldiers whisper. "Sometimes she takes the shape of an owl . . . sometimes a bird of ill omen. . . ."

All glance about them nervously, peering into the shadowy corners of the dark hall. Suddenly the clock strikes midnight. With a cry of fear, the soldiers leap up and bar the castle doors.

Scene Two. Leonora and her friend, Inez, steal through the dark, silent garden of the palace. "Why do you insist on this foolhardy adventure?" Inez whispers fearfully. "How did you ever come to love this man?"

"You remember the unknown knight in black whom I crowned victor of the tournament," answers Leonora. "He disappeared when the civil war broke out between Aragon and Biscay, but one night I heard a voice below my balcony, singing a song of love. It was he, my beloved, whom I seek tonight."

"But this is madness," cries Inez. "All the mystery surrounding this

"I come from the mountains, seeking my son," says Azucena.

man makes me fearful of evil to come. Promise that you will forget him."

"Never!" exclaims Leonora. "I love him!"

They go within to await the coming of the knight. A moment later a man makes his way through the deserted garden. Pausing, he gazes up at the lighted window of Leonora's chamber. It is the count. "Ah, Leonora," he whispers passionately, "when will you become my bride?"

Suddenly a melancholy voice sounds through the night. "On this lonely earth I ask the love of only one heart," sings the unknown.

"The troubadour!" mutters di Luna furiously.

Leonora has also heard, and, rushing into the garden, she throws herself into the arms of the man lurking beneath her window. Di Luna presses her to him ardently; in the darkness she has mistaken the count for her lover.

Just then the troubadour pushes through the shrubbery. Confused and horrified, Leonora shrinks back from the count. "It is you alone that I love," she cries, turning to the stranger. In jealous rage di Luna challenges his rival to tell his name.

Raising his visor, the troubadour reveals that he is Manrico, an enemy knight in the service of Biscay. "Why don't you call out the guards and have me seized?" he taunts, as the count starts back.

"You shall die," answers di Luna grimly. "But by my hand. Your fate was sealed when she declared her love for you."

In vain Leonora tries to separate them. Drawing their swords, the rivals cross blades in mortal combat.

ACT TWO, *Scene One.* A band of gypsies are encamped in the mountains of Biscay. It is not long after dawn, but already the men are setting to work at their anvils, and soon a lusty song rings through the glade:

Manrico lies beside the dying embers of the campfire, watching the smiths at their work. Victor in the duel with Count di Luna, he had spared his rival's life, but the treacherous noble sent troops after him and he had been left for dead on the battlefield at Pelila. Azucena found him there, and, carrying the young man to the gypsy camp, she nursed him back to health. Manrico looks at her fondly.

The gypsy is staring at the fire with wild eyes as though she saw some terrible picture in the dying embers. "How fiercely the flames glow," she mutters:

"A lawless mob surges around the poor woman, clamoring for her death. They tie her to the stake . . . the flames rise to heaven. . . . Ah, vengeance, vengeance!"

One of the men calls out that it is time to go to the village, and the gypsies go off singing. When they are alone, Manrico turns to Azucena.

"Who was that woman you were speaking of?" he asks.

"She was my mother," answers the gypsy mournfully. "Accused of bewitching the Count di Luna's little brother, she was burned at the stake.

She begged me to avenge her, and so I stole the baby, meaning to throw him into the flames with her. But as I stood by the fire, a sudden dizziness came over me, and hardly knowing what I did I flung the child in my arms into the flames. Then I turned. . . ." Azucena stares madly before her. "There on the ground lay the count's brother," she shrieks. "I had killed my own child!"

Manrico shrinks back in horror. "But if you killed your own son," he stammers, "then who am I?"

"You are my son." snaps Azucena hastily. "Did I not bring you up? Did I not rescue you when you fell a victim to the count's treachery? O, why did you spare him when you had him in your power?"

"I scarcely know myself." the young man answers. "But it seemed as though some inner voice told me not to kill that man."

"Next time obey me and slay him," the gypsy cries savagely.

Ruiz. a friend of Manrico, hastens up the slope and hands him a letter. It is from Prince Urgel of Biscay, and instructs the young man to go at once and take command of the fortress of Castellor, which has been captured from the enemy. "Also, I must inform you," the message reads, "that news of your supposed death at Pelila has reached the Lady Leonora, and she plans to enter the Della Croce Convent tonight."

Manrico looks up wildly. "Saddle me a horse," he says to Ruiz, snatching up his helmet, sword, and buckler. Azucena implores him not to go. "The convent is in enemy country," she protests. "Why risk this mad adventure?"

"I cannot lose her," he answers. "Farewell, dearest Mother!" With a last embrace, he rushes off down the mountain.

Scene Two. The shadows of evening lengthen over the Della Croce Convent: two men, who have concealed themselves near the entrance, stir impatiently. "It is a daring act to rob the cloister," whispers Ferrando.

"Perhaps," Count di Luna retorts, "but my boldness is prompted by love and wounded pride. No, Leonora, the convent is not for you. . . ."

A bell is heard in the distance. "Quick, station your men yonder," commands the count. "We shall snatch her before she can reach the altar."

Accompanied by her devoted attendant, Inez, Leonora approaches through the gathering dusk. "Life in the world holds no more joys for me," she sighs. "Manrico is dead. But someday we shall be together again, and till then I will spend my days in prayer. . . ."

"No, by Heaven, you shall not!" cries a harsh voice, and in a moment the bewildered women are surrounded by the count's men. Di Luna rushes toward Leonora. But before he can carry off his prize, an armed warrior leaps into their midst. It is the troubadour. Leonora stares at him in joyful amazement, and for the moment the count shrinks back from the rival whom he had thought dead and out of his way forever. Manrico wastes not a moment. Urging his men to attack, he seizes Leonora and bears her off to safety as the rival bands turn the peaceful cloister into a bloody battlefield.

ACT THREE, *Scene One*. The troops of Aragon are encamped about the fortress of Castellor. Di Luna has pitched his tent in a near-by field, and, as the soldiers amuse themselves with games of dice, the count stares up at the battlements. "She is there—in the arms of my rival," he mutters grimly. "But I will part them. . . ."

Ferrando hastens in with the news that a gypsy woman has been caught prowling about the camp. Fearing that she may be a spy, the soldiers drag her before the count.

"Where do you come from?" di Luna asks his captive.

"From the mountains of Biscay," she answers. "I am seeking my son."

Ferrando has been staring at her. He seizes the count's arm. "Hold that fiend," he cries. "She is the murderess of your brother."

Di Luna springs to his feet. "She shall burn!" he shouts hoarsely. "Bind her tightly, men." Azucena writhes in pain.

"O, Manrico," she moans. "Come and save your wretched mother."

"The mother of Manrico!" Di Luna turns on her in savage joy. "Through you I shall at last be revenged."

Scene Two. Within the fortress, preparations are being made for the wedding of Manrico and Leonora. The bride is troubled by the signs of coming battle, and Manrico is forced to admit that the enemy will probably attack the next day. "But do not fear, beloved," he comforts her. "We shall drive them back, and the thought that you are my wife will give me fresh strength." Drawing her to him, he leads her toward the chapel.

Suddenly Ruiz rushes in. "They have captured your mother, Manrico," he gasps. "Already they are preparing to burn her at the stake."

"What!" shouts the troubadour in horror. "Ruiz, gather the men. We must save her." Hastening to a window, he gazes out at the enemy soldiers, who are building a great fire on the plain below. "Barbarians!" he rages. "I will quench your fire with your own blood!"

Drawing his sword, he rushes from the fortress at the head of his men.

ACT FOUR. *Scene One.* Lighted by a torch, two figures make their way cautiously through the dark courtyard of the Aliaferia palace. "This is the place," whispers Ruiz. "The prisoners are kept in the tower yonder. He must be among them."

"Then leave me. I may be able to save him yet," answers his companion. It is Leonora. Manrico's efforts to rescue his mother have failed, and now he lies captive in the dungeon of the count's palace, awaiting his doom. Leonora gazes up sadly. "If only the night breezes would carry my love to you, dearest," she sighs.

As if in answer, the mournful sound of voices chanting a *Miserere* for those about to die echoes in the still night. Leonora shudders. Then she starts, and stares upward breathlessly as the voice of her lover floats from the tower above. "Ah, death," he sings, "why do you come so slowly to those who long to die? Farewell, my Leonora. Never forget me."

"How could I forget you?" she cries in anguish. "Beloved, I shall save your life at the cost of my own or else die with you."

The door of the palace opens and the count appears on the threshold. Leonora slips back into the shadows. "At sunrise the troubadour is to be beheaded and his mother burned," di Luna instructs his officers.

Then, turning, he comes out into the night. "It is Leonora who drives me to these deeds of vengeance," he mutters. "But alas, I have lost her. All my efforts to trace her since the fall of Castellor have been in vain. Ah, where are you, heartless one?"

"I am here," cries a voice in the shadows, and, flinging herself on her knees before the count, Leonora implores him to spare Manrico.

Di Luna repulses her in jealous fury. "Are you mad?" he shouts. "Shall I spare my bitterest foe? No. Since you have pleaded for him, his sufferings shall be multiplied a hundred fold." He turns to go, but Leonora catches at his cloak in desperation.

"Wait," she begs. "If you will release Manrico, I will become your wife."

The count stops short. "Do you swear it?" he demands eagerly.

She nods. "There is only one condition. You must let me go to his cell and set him free. After that you may claim me."

"Then I promise to spare him." Filled with joy at the thought of possessing Leonora, the count does not see her open the ring she is wearing and put it to her lips. "Come, let us go in," he cries triumphantly. "At last you shall be mine."

Scene Two. Azucena has been thrust into the dungeon with her son, and lies exhausted on a heap of rags at one side. "Are you asleep, Mother?" he whispers. But she is not asleep. Visions of the past fill her wandering mind, and once again she sees the terrible picture of her mother, burning to death at the stake. Now she is to be the next victim. "Save me, Manrico," she shrieks. He tries to comfort her.

"Rest. Mother dear," he pleads.

"Yes, I will rest," she mutters. "We will go back to the peace of our mountains. . . ."

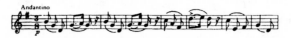

As she drops off to sleep, Leonora appears in the doorway. "You are free, Manrico," she whispers. "Hurry, my love, you must go immediately."

"Are you not coming with me?" he cries, embracing her ardently.

"No, I must stay here."

Manrico stares at her in dread. "Look me in the eye," he demands. "Tell me how you obtained my freedom." She does not answer and he thrusts her from him violently. "So you have sold your love to my rival," he raves. "Away from me, traitoress. I despise you. I curse you!"

"No, not that," she falters. "Manrico, take back your curse. . . ." She has become deathly pale, and sinks slowly to the ground as if paralyzed. Manrico catches her in his arms with a cry of despair.

"How fast the poison works," she murmurs weakly. "Forgive me . . . Manrico. . . ." With a sigh, she slumps back.

The count appears in the doorway. In a flash he understands what has happened, and furiously orders his soldiers to take the troubadour to the execution block. Then, dragging Azucena to the window, he forces her to look out. "See!" he shouts. "Your son has perished!"

A gleam of savage triumph lights the old gypsy's face. "My son?" she shrieks madly. *"No! He was your brother!* . . . Mother, you are avenged!"

Biographical Notes

LUDWIG VAN BEETHOVEN was born in Bonn, Germany, in 1770, and in 1792 went to Vienna, where he remained the rest of his life. At first he was known chiefly as a pianist, but around 1800 he began to write his famous symphonies, and, as he gradually became deaf, he gave up his playing almost entirely. In *Fidelio,* his only opera, he tried to unite voice and orchestra. It was first produced in 1805, was given again with changes in the following year, and appeared in its present form in 1814. Beethoven died in 1827, mourned by all Vienna.

GEORGES BIZET was born in Paris in 1838. *Carmen,* the only one of his works to make a deep impression, was not successful at its première in Paris (1875), but within a few years it had been performed all over the world. Bizet died in Bougival in 1875, three months after *Carmen's* first performance, unaware that his opera was to become a universal favorite.

GAETANO DONIZETTI was born in Bergamo, Italy, in 1797, and died there in 1848. He joined the army to escape being obliged to study law, and while stationed at Venice began to compose operas, soon winning freedom from military duties. His best works, *L'Elisir d'Amore* and *Lucia di Lammermoor,* are full of the graceful melodies and vocal flourishes so natural to the Italians. *Lucia* was first heard in Naples, in 1835.

CHRISTOPH WILLIBALD VON GLUCK was born in Erasback, Upper Palatinate, Germany, in 1714. He began his career as an operatic composer in Italy, writing, after the fashion of the day, operas whose purpose was mainly to show off the singers' voices. It was not until he was nearly fifty that, under the influence of the poet, Calzabigi, and others at the Vienna Court Opera, Gluck made the dramatic reforms for which he is famous, and which first appeared in *Orfeo* (1762). This opera was first given in Vienna where, in 1787, Gluck died.

CHARLES-FRANÇOIS GOUNOD was born at Paris in 1818, and died there in 1893. *Faust* is his masterpiece. Produced in Paris in 1859, this lovely lyric work brought its composer world-wide fame, but, excepting *Romeo et Juliette* (1867), Gounod's other operas have had little effect.

ENGELBERT HUMPERDINCK was born near Bonn, Germany, in 1854. He became a friend of Wagner, and went to Bayreuth, where he helped with the première of *Parsifal.* His own operas, *Hansel and Gretel* (1893) and *Königskinder,* are based on folk tales. He died at Neustrelitz in 1921.

RUGGIERO LEONCAVALLO, like Mascagni, wrote only one really successful opera. Born in Naples in 1858, he earned his living as a café pianist. *Pagliacci* was produced with sensational acclaim at Milan in 1892, and soon appeared on opera stages throughout the world. The composer died at Montecatini in 1919.

PIETRO MASCAGNI was born in Leghorn, Italy, in 1863. He was an orchestral conductor in Cerignola when, in 1890, the production of his one-act opera, *Cavalleria Rusticana*, which had won first prize in a contest, lifted him to sudden fame. None of Mascagni's later works has equalled this first success.

WOLFGANG AMADEUS MOZART was born in Salzburg, Austria, in 1756. As a child he toured the courts of Europe, astonishing his listeners by his wonderful playing of the harpsichord. When he was older he wrote symphonies and operas. Audiences were tired of opera about gods and goddesses, and wanted to hear about people like themselves. In France. where the Revolution threatened. Beaumarchais had even written a play glorifying the common man at the expense of the nobility. So Mozart wrote operas about tradesfolk, peasants, and counts, making his characters life-like and appealing. His *Marriage of Figaro* (1786), *Don Giovanni* (1787), and *Magic Flute* (1791) are among the operatic masterpieces of the world. Never able to find a post worthy of his genius, Mozart was desperately poor all his life, and at his death, in 1791, he was buried in a pauper's grave.

GIOACCHINO ROSSINI, born in Pesaro, Italy, in 1792, was a successful opera composer by the time he was twenty-one. His best-known work, *The Barber of Seville*, was hissed at its first performance (Rome, 1816), but triumphed the second night and soon was heard all over Europe. Rossini was director of the Naples Opera for a time, then lived in Paris, where he presented his masterpiece, *Guillaume Tell* (1829). He died in 1868.

BEDŘICH SMETANA, known as the father of Bohemian music, was born in Leitomischl in 1824. As a young man he accepted a conducting post in Gothenburg, Sweden. In 1860, when Austria granted Bohemia political freedom. Smetana came home to conduct at the new National Opera House. His early works had not been successful, but his opera *The Bartered Bride* (1866), which is full of Czech folk melodies, won him wide fame, and he was acclaimed as Bohemia's greatest composer. He died, stone deaf, in an asylum at Prague in 1884.

GIUSEPPE VERDI, born near Busseto, Italy, in 1813, began as a conventional Italian operatic composer. He gave himself whole-heartedly to voicing in music the Italian national aspirations for independence from the Austrian yoke; in some of his early works he shows the hatred of the Italians for their rulers. *Rigoletto* (1851) began a period of creative brilliance, including such popular operas as *Il Trovatore* (1853), *La Traviata* (1853), *Simon Boccanegra, Ballo in Maschera*, and *La Forza del Destino;* in all of these Verdi's wonderful gift of melody is everywhere to be seen. He was much influenced by Wagner and by the poet-composer, Arrigo Boïto, yet his development was always independent. In *Aïda* (1871), his harmony